COLLECTOR'S GUIDE TO
BASEBALL
CARDS

Wallace-Homestead Collector's Guide™ Series
Harry L. Rinker, Series Editor

COLLECTOR'S GUIDE TO
BASEBALL
CARDS

TROY KIRK

Wallace-Homestead Collector's Guide™ Series

Wallace-Homestead Book Company
Radnor, Pennsylvania

Copyright © 1990 by Troy Kirk
All Rights Reserved
Published in Radnor, Pennsylvania 19089, by Wallace-Homestead Book Company

Designed by Anthony Jacobson
Manufactured in the United States of America

Cover
Design by Anthony Jacobson; photograph by Jim Conroy; baseball jersey courtesy of Peter Capolino,
Mitchell & Ness Notalgia Co., Philadelphia; baseball cards from the collection of Don Poppe, Whitehall,
Pa.

Library of Congress Cataloging in Publication Data

Kirk, Troy.
    A collector's guide to baseball cards / Troy Kirk.
        p.   cm.—(Wallace-Homestead collector's guide series)
    Includes bibliographical references (p.).
    ISBN 0-87069-533-9 (pbk.)
    1. Baseball cards—Collectors and collecting—United States.
I. Title. II. Series.
GV875.3.K57   1990
769'.49796357'0973—dc20   89-51554
                                                                              CIP

2 3 4 5 6 7 8 9 0   8 7 6 5 4 3 2 1

To
Carlye

Contents

CONTENTS

Chapter 4: The Organized Hobby   71

Chapter 5: Building a Collection   89

Chapter 6: Using Price Guides to Follow the Market   105

Chapter 7: Profiting from Baseball Cards   115

Chapter 8: The Future   135

Appendixes 143

Index 152

Preface

I first became aware of the world of baseball cards when I was a seven-year-old growing up in Michigan in the mid-1960s. A friend showed me his collection, carefully stored in an old shoebox. I had never seen or heard of such a thing as baseball cards, and I wasn't much of a baseball fan, but I was immediately hooked. My friend indicated that he might be willing to part with some of his cards, but he told me he would never trade his prize card—one picturing a Detroit Tiger player named Willie Horton. I immediately wanted the card, but I didn't know why it was so prized until he told me it was because Horton played for our home team, the Tigers. From that moment on, I have been a rabid Detroit Tiger fan.

When I started my baseball card collection, I did anything I could to acquire new cards. I had very little money, so I had to purchase cards when I could and use them wisely in trades with my friends. I think I probably convinced all my friends to collect cards so I would have a bigger pool of cards available for trades. Back then, there was nothing I would rather do than trade baseball cards. My usual strategy was to buy a few packs of cards and hopefully get a couple of Tiger duplicates. I would then invite all of my baseball card–collecting friends over for a trading session. I would pull out my new Tiger duplicates one by one and ask for offers. I could usually get 20 or 30 cards for each Tiger.

In those days, there was no interest in rookie cards and very little interest in superstar cards. The only cards we really wanted were Tigers. I can remember one lucky day when I pumped five nickels into a baseball card machine (kind of like a slot machine), turned the knob, and pulled out two 1968 cards of Al Kaline, among others. This was like hitting the jackpot, because Kaline was the all-time great Tiger. I immediately ran home and called my friends to set up a trading session. I remember trading one Kaline card in what I thought was a fantastic deal. Then another friend offered me almost 200 cards for my other Kaline. I had a steadfast rule never to trade any cards other than duplicates, but I waived the rule in this case. It was just too many cards to pass up. I remember being happy about the trade but still having misgivings about having to give up both Kaline cards. After trading my second Kaline, I remember thinking that I'd have to try to find someone else to trade with to get another Ka-

Fig. 1. Two cards from the author's youth: 1966 Topps Willie Horton and 1968 Topps Al Kaline. Copyright The Topps Company, Inc.

line. I kicked myself many times during the next six years before I obtained another 1968 Kaline card (Fig. 1).

I can remember cards being available in several ways in my boyhood days of the late 1960s. You could get them in gum packs at five cards for a nickel or from a machine at the same rate of five cards for a nickel but with no gum. There were also rack packs available that contained approximately 50 cards, but they were way too expensive for me back then (probably around 50 cents). I usually bought the cards at drugstores in my area.

Back in the sixties, the name Topps meant baseball cards. Occasionally I would hear of baseball cards being produced by other companies, but The Topps Company was the company that made big sets of cards every year. Topps made its cards available in seven different series at that time. This meant that in April only the first series of about 100 cards was available. No matter how many packs of cards you bought, you were only going to get cards numbered from 1 to 100. By the time the sixth and seventh series should have been available, the stores would often have football

cards or unsold packs of earlier series. Because of this, the high series were often very difficult to get and always seemed to be in short supply. The scarcity of high-numbered cards that was observable then has been verified over time—high-number cards are usually a lot scarcer now than the other cards from the same sets.

In the 1960s and early 1970s, Topps would usually include an insert in packs of cards from certain series. Topps would not put inserts in first series cards because the company knew that the kids would be so glad just to see the cards that they didn't need any extra incentive to buy them. By about the third or fourth series, Topps would usually start putting inserts in the packs. The inserts were usually a smaller baseball card, a poster, a sticker, a coin, or something similar. Topps was very creative with its use of inserts in those days. There were a smaller number of inserts in a complete insert set than there were in a complete regular set of cards. I sometimes even tried to put together a complete set of the inserts, something that I thought was impossible to do with the regular set.

When I first began collecting baseball cards, I had no idea that any adults collected cards or that there were people who were involved in organized baseball card collecting and who sponsored newsletters and get-togethers whose sole purpose was the buying, selling, and trading of baseball cards. When I first realized in the early 1970s that these organized aspects existed, I was amazed. I began subscribing to some of the baseball card hobby publications (none of which exist today), such as *The Trader Speaks, Sports Collectors News, Sports Scoop,* and some other similarly unstable magazines. These publications were vital for obtaining any information about baseball cards other than information available by going to local stores and looking for cards. There were no baseball card price guides and no books that I could find about cards in existence. Since the card magazines often went out of business, it was risky to send for subscriptions. I usually only subscribed to the ones with the most professional appearance, and I didn't lose much money.

Soon after I first learned of the organized card-collecting world, I received word that there would be a baseball card convention at a local high school. It was to be the first Northern California baseball card convention (my family had moved to California in 1970). I immediately told my two card-collecting buddies, Mark and Rich, about the show, and we all planned to go. We didn't really know what it would be like, but we had great expectations. We weren't disappointed. We were overwhelmed by all the old baseball cards available and the low prices. We had each brought what we considered a sizable amount of money, and each of us had spent it all within a few hours. If we hadn't been hooked on baseball cards before, we certainly were after going to that show.

From then until now I have continued to collect baseball cards. In the time I have collected, card collecting has changed in many ways, from the companies that make cards to the tremendous growth of the organized card-collecting hobby. Topps is still out there making new card sets, but the company now has a lot of competition, with several other major companies producing large baseball card sets each year. In addition, there are now more than 100 smaller sets produced annually.

There is much more information available to baseball card collectors these days than there was in the past. The baseball card magazines are now very professional, with large circulations and many advertisers virtually guaranteeing their continued success. There are many price guides available to help collectors get accurate price information on just about

any card ever made. The price guides are not only useful for information about card values, but they are also valuable checklists for almost all the card sets ever produced.

There are numerous baseball card shows held throughout the country each year. In some major cities, there are card shows almost every weekend. In addition to the many local shows, there is also a National Convention that is held in a different part of the country every year. The National Convention has grown immensely since its inception in 1980. There are usually well over 10,000 people attending the show and over 400 card dealers.

Probably the biggest changes that have taken place in card collecting over the years are in the level of interest in baseball cards and in the prices cards are now commanding. There have never been so many people involved in card collecting as there are today. Prices of baseball cards have been rising so fast that people are now hoarding large quantities of new cards as soon as they are issued, for investment purposes.

I have written this book for two reasons. The first is because I love baseball cards and want to present a salute to the cards themselves. The second reason is that there is still an information gap about baseball card collecting. Although there are numerous price guides telling collectors what is available and what the current values are, there is very little information available about the history of baseball cards and card collecting, historical price trends, card distribution, factors influencing card values, and other information that is presented in this book. This book is intended to provide card collectors and investors with the information that is missing in the price guides, so collecting and investing in baseball cards can be even more fun and profitable.

I hope you enjoy reading this book as much as I have enjoyed writing it.

Acknowledgments

This book has been made possible through the efforts of all of the baseball card manufacturers and collectors, past and present. I thank the manufacturers for their hard work and dedication in creating all of the beautiful and interesting baseball cards that have been issued so far and all of those that are yet to come. I thank the collectors for saving and preserving the cards, making it possible for new generations of collectors to enjoy the cards of the past. Special thanks go to those collectors who have shared their knowledge of the hobby with others by cataloguing cards, writing articles, and publishing baseball card reference books.

Thanks go to Lionel Carter, one of the great old-time collectors and hobby writers, who has helped tremendously in sharing his knowledge and his time; to Larry Fritsch, Lew Lipset, Richard Gelman, Dr. Keith H. Brodie, and Andrea Neuman for their help in locating some of the pictures for his book; to Andrea Bayer of the Metropolitan Museum of Art for letting a desperate collector and author in to see the fabulous Jefferson Burdick collection on very short notice; and to the Onondaga Historical Association of Syracuse, New York, for help in gathering information. Thanks also go to the executives of Topps, Fleer, Donruss, Optigraphics, Upper Deck, O-Pee-Chee, Collectors Marketing Corp., and Pacific Trading Cards who generously provided me with information about their companies and offered other important help.

Most of the pictures in this book were taken by Nancy Christensen, and I thank her for the quality work and cheerful attitude she brought to this project. I am also grateful to all of my friends and relatives who have generously helped me with my baseball card collection over the years and have put up with my baseball card addiction. In particular, I thank lifelong friends and fellow collectors Mark A. Larson and Rich Sawyer. Special thanks and love go to my Mom and Dad for their continuous support through the years.

Introduction

The reason baseball card collecting has been going on for so long and is even bigger today than ever before is because it is *fun*. There are so many different baseball cards available that there is no such thing as a complete collection of baseball cards. There is always something new to search for. Collecting baseball cards is an ongoing search for treasure. You never know when you'll stumble across something rare, valuable, uncatalogued, or just the last card you need to complete a set.

The thrill of collecting in general is in searching for something nobody else has or putting together a unique collection of some particular items from a field of interest. Baseball card collecting is richer in the things a collector looks for than just about any other hobby. Baseball card collecting is affordable to all, there is a wide variety of interesting items available, there are challenges in finding some of the scarcer cards, and there is the rich history of baseball over the past century to draw and hold the interest of collectors.

Pricing

Baseball card collecting is a hobby that everyone can afford. Every year the baseball card companies put out new sets of cards, with each card costing only pennies. One of the major markets is young boys, and the pricing is set so that they can afford to buy baseball cards. Since children are among the poorest people in the country, it follows that even people with a limited amount of spending money can afford to have a baseball card collection.

There is a wide price range for older baseball cards. Most people can afford samples of even the oldest baseball cards, though accumulating quantities of old cards can become very expensive. For people who want a challenge, baseball card collecting is an interesting hobby because some cards are extremely difficult to find at any price. There are also some glamour cards that carry a high price tag, but are obtainable. Baseball card collecting holds something of interest for people with just about any budget.

Variety

Baseball cards have been issued for over 100 years by many different companies. There have been over 1,000 different baseball card sets released. Within each set, there are many different individual cards. In recent years, more than 100 new sets have been issued each year.

It is a reasonable guess to say that more than 100,000 different baseball cards exist today. With so many different baseball cards and baseball card sets available, there is enough variety to satisfy any collector.

Color and Artwork

Baseball card sets have always been designed with the collector in mind. Card companies have constantly tried to produce cards with the newest photography and printing technologies, the most colorful and innovative card designs, and the most interesting choice of subjects.

Photography and Printing Processes

The color and artwork of baseball cards have always reflected the latest developments in photography and printing processes. The earliest baseball cards of the 1880s look like some of the earliest photographs that were ever made. They are in a brown-and-white tone (sepia) and, like many photographs of that era, are often found to be faded today. The pictures themselves reflect the fashion of the times, with the subjects in very posed situations. Most of the pictures were taken in a studio. Many of the players have large moustaches, which was the fashion for men in the United States in the 1880s.

As time went on, baseball cards were printed in color, often with very colorful backgrounds. Many of the baseball cards of the 1910 era consist of black-and-white photographs that were printed and then colored, since color photography did not exist at that time. Some other cards from the same era consist of line drawings done using player photographs as models.

It wasn't until the early 1950s that color photographs were first used to create baseball cards. For the first time, baseball cards of players were exact images of the subjects (Fig. I-1).

In the late 1960s and 1970s, some 3-D style baseball cards were created. Kellogg's cereal produced an annual 3-D baseball card set from 1970 through 1983. These cards have a ridged plastic coating to make the subject appear to be moving as the card is turned at different angles. A similar technology was used by SportFlics beginning in 1986 to produce baseball cards that show three different pictures when turned at different angles.

Card Designs

There has always been a lot of innovation in the design of baseball cards. Most baseball cards have some type of artistic design, as well as some identifying text printed on the front of the cards along with the picture of the subject. The front designs have often combined color and creativity to produce beautiful and

Fig. I-1. Baseball cards through the years: 1887 Old Judge Larry Twitchell, 1910 American Caramel George Gibson, 1950 Bowman Owen Friend, 1970 Topps Tom Seaver, 1988 Topps Harold Baines. Topps cards copyright The Topps Company, Inc.

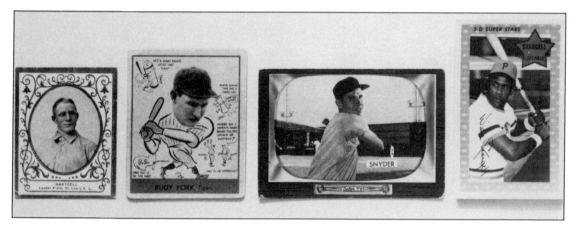

Fig. I-2. Baseball cards with interesting front designs: 1909 Ramly Tobacco Roy Hartzell, 1938 Goudey Rudy York, 1955 Bowman Jerry Snyder, 1971 Kellogg's Willie Stargell.

interesting cards. Each year the card companies create their cards with a new design (Fig. I-2).

The backs of the cards are usually informative and have often been very innovative, too. Modern baseball card backs usually contain complete or recent statistics for the pictured player. Many of them include an informative biography of the player's accomplishments. There are often special features on the backs; for example, many Topps cards sport small cartoons that tell stories of past feats by the player. The 1964 Topps card backs have a trivia question on the bottom of the card; the answer was found by scratching off a blank box on the card with a coin. The backs of the 1987 Fleer cards have a special feature that gives a chart of the strengths and weaknesses of the player pictured.

The card backs for older baseball card sets

Fig. I-3. Some interesting advertising designs on baseball card backs: 1947 Sunbeam bread, 1910 Red Sun cigarettes, 1909–1911 Polar Bear cigarettes.

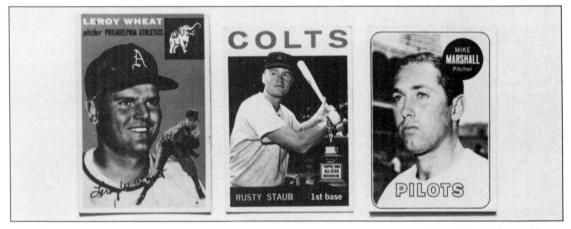

Fig. I-4. Cards featuring teams that no longer exist: 1954 Topps Leroy Wheat of the Philadelphia Athletics (now Oakland A's), 1964 Topps Rusty Staub of the Houston Colts (now Houston Astros), 1969 Topps Mike Marshall of the Seattle Pilots (now Milwaukee Brewers). Topps cards copyright The Topps Company, Inc.

were usually used for advertising purposes. For example, the Red Sun cigarettes cards (1910) contain an ad on the back that is very attractive. It pictures a red sun rising with the Red Sun logo. Most of the tobacco cards of the 1909–1915 era have front designs that are paired with a variety of back designs, because these cards were issued simultaneously with many different brands of cigarettes. Each brand has its own unique back design, many of which are very interesting (Fig. I-3).

Choice of Subjects

The choice of subjects often shows signs of the times. For example, the 1880s Old Judge tobacco set contains several cards of players pictured with a team mascot. The Red Cross tobacco and Cracker Jack candy sets of 1915 show cards of some players pictured with the short-lived Federal League. The Federal League was a third major league that existed from 1914 to 1915. Many sets show players from teams that have moved, dating the cards to a particular era. There have often been small sets created to show only the subjects of the most recent World Series winning team. In some sets, multiple cards are produced for star players while lesser players only merit one card. There are cards picturing several of the current superstars of baseball together. The Topps cards created for expansion teams in their first year usually have airbrushed caps and uniforms for the players, since no existing pictures of the players with their new teams are available when the sets are being prepared (Fig. I-4).

The Thrill of the Hunt

Probably the best thing about collecting baseball cards is searching for cards and uncovering hidden treasures. Just about every collector dreams of uncovering a collection of old, rare, and perhaps even uncatalogued baseball cards. This can be done. In recent years, the following items have been uncovered by collectors:

- Most of an unopened case of 1952 Topps high-numbered cards, worth hundreds of thousands of dollars.
- A large collection of baseball discs issued with Ju Ju Drums candy from 1910, including some discs that were previously uncatalogued.
- An old trunk containing many Turkey Reds and Old Judge tobacco cards. The cards from this find are worth thousands of dollars.

In addition, many other rare and valuable cards have also been found by collectors. It is not necessary to find very rare cards to experience the thrill of uncovering hidden treasures. There can be an equal thrill in finding the new cards at the store, or in finding some old cards for sale at a bargain price at a flea market or swap meet, or in finding cards in a number of other ways. (Some good places to find cards and strategies for getting them at a reasonable price are discussed later in this book.)

Baseball and Its Players

Baseball card collecting is tied to the game of baseball itself. Almost since its invention, baseball has been the U.S. national pastime. Baseball has a massive following in the United States, from children playing Little League, to adults playing softball, to people of all ages actively following their favorite professional baseball teams. Its rich history stretches back over 100 years and is very well chronicled. There have been many famous and colorful personalities throughout the history of baseball, from early stars such as Cap Anson and Cy Young in the late 1800s to early 1900s; to Ty Cobb and Walter Johnson in the early 1900s through the 1920s; to Babe Ruth and Lou Gehrig and their leadership of the Yankee dynasty of the 1920s and 1930s; to Joe DiMaggio and Ted Williams in the 1940s and 1950s; to Mickey Mantle, Willie Mays, Hank Aaron, and Sandy Koufax in the 1950s and 1960s; to Pete Rose and Reggie Jackson in the 1960s though the 1980s; to Dwight Gooden, Don Mattingly, and Jose Canseco in the 1980s and into the 1990s. All of these superstars and thousands of other stars and lesser players have played the game and brought pleasure to millions of fans.

Baseball itself is probably the "fairest" of all of the professional team sports that are played in the United States. Baseball players more closely resemble everyday people than do players in sports such as basketball, in which players are usually very tall, or football, in which players are usually very large. Baseball players must master many skills in order to make it to the big leagues, but size is not as big a factor as it is in other sports. Baseball is also the only major team sport that does not rely on a clock to end a game. There is always a chance to win the game up until the very last out is made. There have been numerous occasions when a team staged a last-inning rally to win a game, sometimes coming back from many runs behind. In basketball and football, the game can be over before the clock says the game has ended. Baseball is played in a relaxed summer atmosphere and moves at its own pace. There is a lot of anticipation and strategy in baseball, and, while some critics have attacked it as being boring, baseball fans never doubt the greatness of the sport. Those who find it boring are usually the ones who have the least knowledge of the game. The long baseball season is perfect for measuring which teams really deserve to win at the end. The baseball playoff structure has traditionally allowed only the top teams to play for the championship. Baseball has been fair in rewarding the teams that have proven themselves over the long season.

Baseball has remained practically the same game since its very beginnings. Today's game is played with essentially the same rules that have been in effect for over a century. The game is unique in that there are meaningful statistics kept on every player. Because of this, it is possible to compare players from past eras with today's players. *The Baseball Encyclopedia,* edited by Joseph Reichler and published by Macmillan, lists every player who has ever played even one major league game, from the very first days of professional baseball up until the present day. *The Baseball Encyclopedia* lists all players' statistics, along with other information, such as when they were born and died, nicknames, injuries during their careers, whether they had any relatives who played in the majors, and other facts that really make the players come alive. If you get a baseball card of a player you've never heard of, all you need to do is refer to *The Baseball Encyclopedia* to find out exactly who he is.

Consulting *The Baseball Encyclopedia* is especially useful if you want to collect very old baseball cards, such as cards from the nineteenth century or early twentieth century. These cards often only list the name of the player and his team. Not too many people around nowadays remember the players from those eras, so *The Baseball Encyclopedia* is a great way to find out a little about the players pictured on the old cards.

Because its foundations lie in the game of baseball itself, baseball card collecting will continue to be popular in the years ahead. Baseball has thrived through over 100 years of changing times and will continue to thrive because of the basic greatness of the game. This greatness will continue to keep baseball card collecting going through both good and bad times.

Understanding the Terminology

What Are Baseball Cards?

Baseball cards are pictures of anything to do with the game of baseball printed on cardboard or thick paper. The most popular baseball cards are pictures of baseball players, although cards have been issued with umpires, league officials, stadiums, trophies, and important baseball events such as the World Series or All-Star games. There is usually some print on the front and back identifying the subject and sometimes listing statistics or a biography.

Baseball cards have been traditionally issued by manufacturers as a bonus insert that is included with a product; however, in recent years the cards themselves have become the product in more and more cases. Baseball cards have been issued in varying sizes, but they are most commonly found in sizes smaller than a postcard, with a fairly standard current size of 2½″ × 3½″.

Categorizing Baseball Cards

The Need for Categorizing

Baseball cards were first issued in the 1880s as inserts with cigarettes. They were a hit with the public from the beginning, and many different card sets were issued by various manufacturers over the years with cigarettes and other products. By the 1930s, baseball cards had been issued for over 40 years with no reference work available to help collectors know anything about card sets of the past. There were no lists of baseball card sets issued in the past, no checklists for cards within the sets, and no pricing information about any cards. In the 1930s, the rarest baseball cards issued to that date had no special value attached to them, because nobody knew which cards were rare and which were common.

There were people collecting baseball cards at that time, but there was very little shared knowledge about cards because there were no reference books, baseball card hobby magazines, or newsletters. The first published information about baseball cards came in the early 1930s through *Hobbies Magazine,* a publication that presented articles on a variety of hobbies. A man named Jefferson R. Burdick wrote a series of articles for this magazine about early cigarette cards. Based on the response he got from readers of his articles, he realized there was a greater need for information on card issues.

Early Work

In the mid-1930s, Jefferson Burdick began devising a system for categorizing baseball cards and all other types of cards. With the help of collectors from around the country, he amassed as much information as he could find and released this work in a book. Though given a different name originally, it was later titled *The American Card Catalog.* First published in 1939, the book was updated every few years until what turned out to be the last version came out in 1960, three years before Burdick's death. This book was reprinted in 1988 in its exact 1960 form and is available today from the Card Collectors' Company (Fig. 1-1). (The address of the Card Collectors' Company is located in Appendix D of this book.)

In *The American Card Catalog,* Burdick created a system to identify the type of company that was producing a particular set of cards along with the type of subjects pictured. The system Burdick developed for categorizing cards involved giving all sets of cards an alphabetic letter or letters indicating how or when the cards were issued, followed by a number for each specific set. For example, Burdick assigned the code of T206 to one of the most popular sets of baseball cards of all time. The T indicates that this particular set of cards was issued in the twentieth century by a tobacco manufacturer. The 200 series of

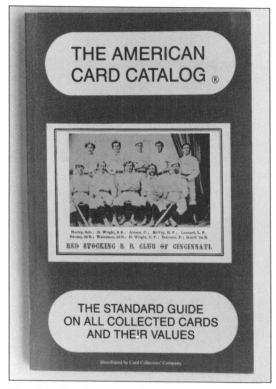

Fig. 1-1. The American Card Catalog *by Jefferson Burdick (1988 reprinted version).*

numbers for T cards indicates that the subjects are sports-oriented. The low 200 numbers are baseball cards.

Most early baseball card sets and other early sets of cards are still known by their *American Card Catalog* code numbers, even though very few of today's collectors own *The American Card Catalog.* Since Burdick's death in 1963, there have been no successful attempts to update *The American Card Catalog* code numbers to include recent baseball cards and other sets. A few people have assigned code numbers to newer sets, but these systems have not caught on with the collecting community. Baseball card sets of today are generally categorized by their manufacturers' names and the year of issue. For example, the designation "Topps 1969 cards" indicates the 664-card set of baseball cards that Topps issued in 1969. Topps issued several other sets and subsets of cards in 1969, but the name "Topps 1969" indicates the company's major issue for that year.

In some ways it is a shame that the work of Jefferson Burdick has not been continued. With over 100 different baseball card sets being issued each year in recent years, along with numerous nonbaseball card sets, it is becoming more and more difficult to keep track of what is available. The baseball card price guides and other sport and non-sport card guides that are available today present a fantastic reference to the sets of cards that have been issued, but space limitations are preventing many sets from being included. If a numbering system such as the one Burdick used were still in place, collectors would at least know when a card set was missing from the price guide. For example, if the guide listed the T204, T205, T206, and T208 sets, readers could guess that there is a set for T207 that was not included. With no numbering system in place today, there is no way for the average collector to guess which sets are not included in today's price guides.

Even though Burdick catalogued card sets up until 1960, his code numbers are really only still used for card sets issued before 1948. The year 1948 is the magic year of the first Bowman issue and really marks the beginning of modern baseball cards. So if you see an *American Card Catalog* code number designating a set of cards, you can be pretty sure it was issued before 1948. The main code letters for baseball cards that Burdick used are as follows:

N   Nineteenth-century baseball cards (Burdick did not originally use an N, but it has been added later to his numbers)
T   Twentieth-century tobacco cards
E   Early candy and gum cards
R   Gum cards from 1933 to the present (in practice, Burdick's numbers are only used from 1933 to 1941)
C   Canadian tobacco cards
V   Canadian gum cards
W   Strip cards, Exhibit cards, team issues
D   Bakery cards
M   Periodical cards
S   Silks
L   Leathers
B   Blankets
F   Food inserts
H   Advertising cards

Here are some examples of catalog numbers assigned to major sets by Burdick along with a brief description of the sets:

N172: Small ($1\frac{1}{2}'' \times 2\frac{1}{2}''$) sepia-toned cards issued by Goodwin & Company with Old Judge and Gypsy Queen cigarettes from 1887–1890; over 2,000 known.

T206: Small ($1\frac{1}{2}'' \times 2\frac{1}{2}''$) color cards issued by the American Tobacco Company with many different brands of cigarettes from 1909–1911; over 500 known.

E90-1: Small ($1\frac{1}{2}'' \times 2\frac{3}{4}''$) color cards issued by the American Caramel Company with its candy from 1908–1912; 120 known.

R319: Medium-sized ($2\frac{3}{8}'' \times 2\frac{7}{8}''$) color cards printed on thick cardboard by the Goudey Gum Company in 1933; 240 known.

Note: The American Card Catalog uses many other letters to designate other types of cards, most of which do not depict baseball subjects. A complete list of *American Card Catalog* identification letters is presented in Appendix A of this book.

Categorization Today

The categorization of baseball cards from 1948 to the present is not as well organized as

Fig. 1-2. National major baseball card issues: 1985 Topps Reggie Jackson, 1989 Score Carney Lansford, 1987 Fleer Carlton Fisk, 1989 Donruss Mike Greenwell. Topps cards copyright The Topps Company, Inc.

the categorization work which had been done by Burdick for earlier cards. However, there are some rules that collectors tend to go by when classifying sets of cards issued in recent years.

National Major Issues

National major issues are the large comprehensive sets that are issued nationwide by the large baseball card manufacturers. Examples include the yearly major sets from Topps, Fleer, Donruss, Score, and SportFlics. These are the sets that almost all baseball card collectors collect (Fig. 1-2). In recent years, Topps, Fleer, Donruss, and Score have been producing over 600 cards in each of their national major issues of baseball cards, picturing most of the active players.

Other National Issues

There are sets that are issued nationally but that either do not contain the scope of or have some physical differences from the major issues. These sets are still avidly collected, but not as much as the major issues. There are many different types of sets that fall into this category. Examples include the Post Cereal issues of 1960–1963, the Hostess cards of 1975–1979, and the Kellogg's cards of 1970–1983. Other examples include sets from companies that only issued cards for one year, including Hires Root Beer in 1958, Milk Duds in 1971, and Quaker Chewy Granola Bars in 1986.

Other nonmajor national issues include all nationally issued subsets of the major sets, such as the 1969 Topps Deckle Edge inserts, the Topps annual write-in bonus glossy cards, the Fleer All-Star cards of 1986 and later, the Topps Glossy Rac-Pac All-Star cards of recent years, the cards found on some wax pack box bottoms, and other similar sets (Fig. 1-3).

Recently, Topps and Fleer have been producing complete boxed sets containing less than 50 cards that they have been issuing exclusively through chain stores. For example, the K-Mart and McCrory chains have sold exclusive boxed sets at their stores throughout the country. These are also nonmajor national issues. In general, any set that is issued nationally that is not one of the major sets falls into this "nonmajor national" category.

Regional Issues

Regional issues are card sets that are sold or distributed to people only in specific regions

Fig. 1-3. Nonmajor national issues: 1969 Topps Deckle Edge Insert Juan Marichal, 1971 Bazooka Hank Aaron, 1978 Hostess Joe Ferguson. Topps cards copyright The Topps Company, Inc.

of the country. These sets often contain cards of players on a specific team and are only distributed in that team's regional territory.

Regional cards are often distributed as inserts for a specific product, usually a food product. For example, some cards of this type would include the A's cards given away with Granny Goose potato chips from 1981 to 1983, the Gardners bread Brewers sets of 1983–1985, the various Burger King restaurant sets of the late 1970s and early 1980s, the Wendy's restaurant Tigers set of 1985, and the Kahn's meats sets of the 1950s and 1960s.

Regionals do not have to contain cards of just one team. Drakes's bakeries in the eastern United States have produced annual sets beginning in 1981 containing cards of star players from various teams. Many boxed sets are now appearing that sell exclusively at stores in a particular region of the country. These include 1987 boxed sets produced for Cumberland Farms stores, Eckerd Drugs, Ben Franklin stores, and others.

Baseball cards that are given out by a major league team at a specific baseball game during the season are another type of regional. Some examples include the Mother's Cookies sets that have been given out in various ballparks since 1983, the Cubs sets that have been

given out through various sponsors beginning in 1982, and the Dodgers police sets that have been given out during the 1980s. Usually cards given out at the ballpark have a sponsor or sponsors. Sometimes the cards are distributed in other ways, too. For example, many police organizations sponsor baseball card sets that are given away at a specific baseball game and are also given to children that meet with police officers. The Granny Goose A's cards issued from 1982 and 1983 could be obtained one at a time in individual packages of potato chips or as a complete set at a specific A's game. The White Sox made its card sets of 1985 and 1986 more difficult to complete by giving away only two cards out of a 30-card set at specific home baseball games. In order to get a complete set, you had to go to 15 different games or do a lot of trading (Fig. 1-4).

In general, regional sets are printed in much smaller numbers than sets that are distributed nationally. They are also collected by a much smaller number of collectors. It is a great challenge to acquire regional sets without going bankrupt. There are some baseball card dealers who sell regionals, but the cards are usually marked up quite a bit. If you buy regional cards from a dealer, you will usually pay approximately double what you would pay if you lived

Fig. 1-4. Regional issues: 1968 Detroit Free Press Norm Cash, 1984 Smokey the Bear Padres Eric Show, 1983 Granny Goose A's Mike Davis.

in the region where the cards appear. In the 1980s, there have been numerous regional sets produced each year, so the cost of acquiring these cards adds up very quickly.

Minor League Issues

There have been many minor league sets of baseball cards produced over the years. In general, they do not command the respect of or attract collectors in the way that cards of major league players do.

Minor league baseball cards have been around since the very first baseball cards were issued. Many minor leaguers were pictured on their own cards along with major leaguers in the very first sets of baseball cards issued in 1887. There were also cards of minor leaguers included in such widely collected early sets as the T206 and T205 tobacco issues. Several of the early tobacco card sets pictured minor leaguers only. For example, the Obak tobacco cards pictured players from the Pacific Coast League in the 1910 era. These cards were widely collected on the West Coast, mainly because there were no major league teams on the West

Coast at the time and no television coverage. The minor league cards were very important during this era because they pictured the only players that could be seen by people living on the West Coast. This was true in many other parts of the country also.

In the modern era of card collecting, there haven't really been any sets that contained both major and minor league players. Bowman put out a small set of Pacific Coast League cards in 1949, but it was separate from Bowman's regular 1949 issue. There have been some regional minor league sets put out, such as Mother's Cookies cards in the early 1950s, and many minor league card sets given away or sold at minor league ballparks. While these sets may be desirable for seeing some players on their way up to the majors or on their way down, the cards are not highly collected (Fig. 1-5).

In the 1970s and 1980s there have been some companies, most notably TCMA (now CMC) and ProCards, who have made it their business to produce baseball card sets of minor leaguers. These sets are usually offered to collectors only through baseball card dealers.

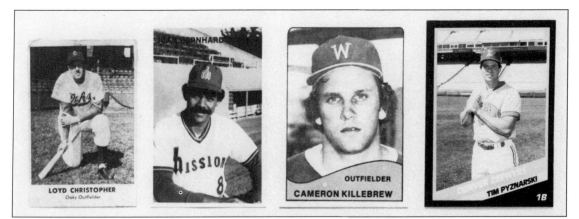

Fig. 1-5. Minor League baseball cards: 1949 Remar Bread Lloyd Christopher, 1978 Mr. Chef's Fish & Chix San Jose Missions Juan Bernhardt, 1979 TCMA Wausau Timbers Cameron Killebrew, 1988 CMC Denver Zephyrs Tim Pyznarski. Cameron Killebrew is the son of Hall of Famer Harmon Killebrew.

Foreign Issues

While baseball cards are found mostly in the United States, some foreign countries have also produced them, most notably Canada. Canada has produced baseball card sets sporadically since the early twentieth century. A minor league tobacco set of the 1910 era known as C46 pictured International League players. The Goudey Gum Company issued many of its U.S. sets of the 1930s in Canada in slightly different versions. Topps has issued Canadian versions of all of its major sets since 1965 through another company, O-Pee-Chee. Donruss issued Canadian versions of its cards under the Leaf name from 1985 to 1988. Some of the cards issued in Canada have French translations for the write-ups, some are written in both English and French, and some are written only in English. Canadian baseball cards are seen fairly frequently in the United States.

Topps cards were issued in different versions for the Spanish market in the late 1950s and 1960s and were distributed in Venezuela. Some of these cards have Spanish text, while others are written only in English. All of them have some differences from the U.S. versions,

although some vary only in minor characteristics such as the color of ink used on the back.

Baseball is very big in Japan, and there are Japanese baseball cards. These cards are rarely seen in the United States. The most common Japanese baseball cards are issued by Calbee Snack Foods and usually come attached to potato chip bags and other snack foods.

Card collecting is very popular in Europe, especially in England. There is not much baseball played in European countries, however, so baseball card sets are virtually unknown in those countries. Most of the card sets found in England feature various general topics, such as animals, transportation, soccer, and numerous other subjects.

In general, baseball card collecting is an American pastime. Baseball cards that have been issued outside of the United States are generally not collected by U.S. collectors (Fig. 1-6).

Collector Issues, Reprints, and Forgeries

Collector issues are sets of cards that have been produced specifically for the baseball card

Fig. 1-6. Foreign cards: 1980s Cricket card of Chris Tavaré (Great Britain), 1989 Calbee Snack Chips Masato Yoshii (Japan), 1967 Topps Lefty Grove (Venezuela), 1986 Leaf Jesse Barfield (Canada). Cricket is a British game similar in some ways to baseball. Topps card copyright The Topps Company, Inc.

collecting hobby. They are sold exclusively through baseball card dealers and are not available to the general public through retail stores other than baseball card stores. Examples of collector issues are the Sport Star Publishing Company (SSPC) baseball card sets of 1975–1977; the Topps, Fleer, and Donruss update sets that are sold exclusively to baseball card dealers; some minor league issues; and any collector-issued set of baseball cards.

Reprints are new printings of old sets of baseball cards and are almost always collector issues. Often they are created for sets that are too rare or too expensive for the average collector to obtain. Most reprints look somewhat different from the originals, usually in size or card stock. Reprints should always be marked as such right on the cards. Reprint cards that are not marked as reprints are counterfeits and are probably the worst thing that has ever happened to card collecting. Because certain cards have become very valuable, people have attempted to make illegal reproductions of them. There is no collector value in counterfeit cards, and the people responsible for making them are subject to criminal prosecution. The subject of counterfeits is discussed more thoroughly in Chapter 8.

Collector issues and reprints are not considered legitimate collectible baseball cards. Legitimate baseball cards are available to everyone, not just to baseball card collectors. While there may be a place for some of these baseball sets, most baseball card collectors don't actively collect them, and many are even opposed to them.

Oddball Items

There are certain baseball collectibles that fall just outside of the definition of true baseball cards. Some of these items picture baseball players but are not printed on small pieces of cardboard. However, since these items are collected by a great many baseball card collectors, they deserve mention here.

Some of the baseball sets that fall into the category of "oddball items" include baseball coin sets, baseball bottle cap sets, baseball cup sets, baseball statue sets, baseball sticker sets, baseball stamp sets, baseball felt pennant sets, baseball pins, baseball leathers, baseball silks, and miniature baseball blankets. All of these materials and more have been used for baseball collectible sets (Fig. 1-7). In addition to these, there are other items that baseball card collectors sometimes collect, including base-

Fig. 1-7. Some "oddball" baseball collectibles: 1930s Our National Game Pin Lou Gehrig, 1969 MLBPA Pin Luis Aparicio, 1969 Topps Stamps Eddie Fisher, 1984 Topps Stickers Frank Viola. Topps items copyright The Topps Company, Inc.

Fig. 1-8. Three different versions of 1962 Topps #139: Babe Ruth, Hal Reniff (pitching), Hal Reniff (portrait). Copyright The Topps Company, Inc.

ball card wrappers, baseball card display boxes, baseball game ticket stubs, baseball pocket schedules, and many other items relating to baseball. A grocery store display for a baseball card set might be considered a collectible oddball item.

Oddball items are often free and are usually interesting. You never know when you will run across them. Many oddball items are not catalogued anywhere, so it is hard to tell what they are worth. Even though they may not fit the exact definition of baseball cards, they enhance any baseball card collection.

Variations

There have been many sets that contain variation cards. Variations exist when a company makes a change in a card after it has already been issued in a set. This creates two different versions for the same card in the set. Variations have been created to correct errors on the original cards, to show a team change for a player, to change artwork, and for other reasons. Fleer created a variation in its 1989 set when it issued a second version of the card of Billy Ripken to cover up an obscenity that was written on his bat handle. Sets are considered complete if they contain *one* version of each card in the set, even if variations exist. In other words, advertisers can and do sell complete sets that contain one version of each card in the set and none of the known variations (Fig. 1-18).

The History of Baseball Cards

The Origins of Baseball

Since baseball cards are dependent on the game of baseball, a brief history of the origins and structure of professional baseball is in order. The origins of the game of baseball are a bit cloudy, with credit being given to many people and cultures. Though baseball itself is an American game, it is based roughly on the English game of rounders. The first chronicled game of baseball was played in the mid-1840s.

The first professional baseball team appeared in 1869. The team was the Cincinnati Red Stockings, and it traveled around the country that year challenging teams in cities everywhere. This team achieved the fantastic record of 56 wins and 1 tie and became famous throughout the United States. In honor of that team, major league baseball schedules the Cincinnati Reds to be the first team to open play each season.

In 1871, the first professional baseball league was formed and was called the National Association of Professional Baseball Players. The National Association lasted five years until widespread gambling and bribery caused its downfall.

In 1876, the National League was formed with stricter rules to protect against the problems of the earlier league. The National League that was formed then is the same National League that exists today, although many of the teams and cities have changed.

In 1882, an opposing league called the American Association was formed. There were struggles for players and attendance for a couple of years until a truce was called between the two leagues. In 1884, the first postseason series between league champions was played. The American Association lasted until 1891, when it ceased operations. During the years of the American Association's existence, a couple of other short-lived leagues were formed and also folded. From 1892 through 1900, the National League existed as the only major league.

In 1901, the American League was formed, and it has remained in existence to the present day as a second major league. The first modern World Series was played in 1903; the World Series was skipped in 1904 because of trouble between the two leagues and then resumed in

1905. It has been played every year since. The National League and the American League have coexisted as the only major leagues from 1901 to the present, except for a two-year period in 1914 and 1915 when a third major league called the Federal League was in existence.

Though major league baseball has always been the most publicized and glorified form of professional baseball, minor league baseball has been played throughout the country from the early years of the game and is still being played today. In the early days of baseball, the minor leagues consisted of teams that provided baseball for communities that did not have major league teams. Minor league teams were not affiliated with any major league teams, though they often sold their best players to the majors. The caliber of play in some of the minor leagues in the late-1800s through the mid-1900s was sometimes almost as good as the major leagues. The Pacific Coast League, in particular, had a reputation for being a very good league.

In the late 1940s, major league teams began controlling minor league teams for the purpose of developing talent. Today there are very few minor league baseball teams that are not affiliated with a major league team. Also in the late 1940s, baseball began to be seen nationwide on television. Television brought major league baseball to all of the small communities throughout the nation that could previously only watch minor league action. This caused a decline in interest in minor league baseball, so that now there are far fewer minor leagues than there were at their peak in the 1940s.

The structure of baseball has remained fairly stable from the late 1940s through the present. There are now more major league teams, and there are divisional playoffs before the World Series, but everything else is basically the same.

Chronology of Baseball Card Issues

Baseball cards have been going in and out of style throughout their existence. There have been eras when many issues of baseball cards were available and collecting them was a national craze, and there have been other times when no baseball cards were issued at all. Here is a chronological listing of the baseball cards that have been issued in different eras for the past 100 years.

1887–1890: The Beginnings

The years from 1887 to 1890 made up the first era of baseball cards and card collecting. The first baseball cards ever made were issued in 1887 by various tobacco companies. One of

the most important baseball card issues of all time was the series of cards known as N172, issued as inserts in Old Judge and Gypsy Queen cigarettes by Goodwin & Company of New York from 1887 through 1890. This is still the most comprehensive issue of baseball cards of all time, as Goodwin tried to picture every major league player and most minor leaguers on individual cards. There are over 500 players pictured, and more than 2,300 different cards are known to exist, with more being discovered from time to time. Most players are pictured on several different cards in different poses. There have been 10 or more poses and team variations found for some players (Fig. 2-1).

Fig. 2-1. 1887–1890 Old Judge cards manufactured by Goodwin & Company (N172): 1887 Ned Hanlon, 1888 Chas. Brynan, 1887 Stump Weidman, 1889 Phil Knell, 1888 Ed Knouff. In 1887 every member of the St. Louis baseball team except Ed Knouff signed a petition not to play a black baseball team in an exhibition game. That petition marked the first time a color line was drawn in baseball, a line that would not be broken until Jackie Robinson first played in the majors in 1947. Knouff's refusal to sign the petition was an early voice against the prejudicial actions that kept black players out of baseball for so long.

Many other tobacco companies issued baseball cards and other types of cards in the 1887–1890 time period. Some of the tobacco companies issuing baseball cards included Allen & Ginter, Duke, Kimball, S.F. Hess, Lone Jack, and August Beck & Company. The Allen & Ginter cards were particularly beautiful, featuring high-quality color lithographs of the players. Unfortunately, Allen & Ginter issued only a handful of baseball cards as part of larger card sets featuring sports figures of the era.

One manufacturer, the Green & Blackwell Company of New York (G&B), issued baseball cards with chewing gum. Though this card set was relatively insignificant at the time and the cards are very rarely seen today, this set can be considered the granddaddy of modern baseball cards because it was issued with gum.

Baseball cards from the nineteenth century are very different from those issued today. The cards are generally very small (about 1½" × 2¾") and are printed on very thick cardboard. Cards from the nineteenth century usually consist of either a sepia-toned photograph pasted on a thick piece of cardboard or a color lithograph printed on a thick piece of cardboard.

1891–1908: Quiet Years

There were very few baseball card sets produced from 1891 to 1908. About the only significant card sets produced in this time period were the P.H. Mayo & Brother's tobacco set of 1895 (known as N300) and the Breisch-Williams candy set of 1903 (known as E107).

The N300 set was produced by P.H. Mayo & Brother and issued with the company's cut plug tobacco. The set consists of 48 cards, including several players who did not appear in any other baseball card issues. These cards measure 1⅝" × 2⅞" and consist of black-and-white photos with black borders. Most of the players are pictured in uniform; however, some are shown in street clothes, which is very unusual for a baseball card subject.

The E107 set was produced by the Breisch-Williams Company and was issued with some unknown type of candy. The backs of the cards state that there are 150 different players pictured, although there are at least 158 different cards known (including variations). These cards measure 1⅜" × 2⅝" and consist of black-and-white photos with small white borders. This set is significant because its cards closely re-

Fig. 2-2. 1903–1904 Breisch-Williams (E107) Jimmy Barrett, 1895 Mayo (N300) Bill Hallman (in street clothes), 1895 Mayo (N300) Lave Cross.

semble the style of many of the sets that were to be issued in the 1909–1915 era, so E107 is considered to be the forerunner of those later sets (Fig. 2-2). The P.H. Mayo and the Breisch-Williams sets are very important since they are really the only significant sets produced during this 18-year period in baseball history. Both of these sets are very scarce today.

1909–1915: Baseball Card Boom

The second major era of baseball card collecting took place between 1909 and 1915. Many people consider the baseball card collecting hobby really to have started with the issue of the cards from this time period. As in the first big era of baseball card collecting in the late 1880s, the tobacco companies led the way once again in this second boom period by issuing the greatest variety and quantity of baseball cards. In this period, however, baseball cards were also issued with many other types of products, including candy, bread, and sports magazines.

The T206 Tobacco Set

The most significant baseball card set of the 1909–1915 era is the American Tobacco Company set known as T206, generally thought to have been issued from 1909 to 1911. Cards from this set were issued as inserts for different brands of cigarettes produced by the American Tobacco Company. The cards are small (approximately 1½″ × 2½″), and they are in beautiful color. It was generally thought that there were 523 different cards in the set until the discovery of a 524th variation card was made public in 1987. Most of the major league players and many minor leaguers of the era are pictured, and most of the star players are pictured on more than one card, in different poses. Ty Cobb is pictured on four different cards. The most famous and valuable baseball card (though certainly not the rarest)—the card of Honus Wagner—is from this set. The T206 set stands out above the rest of the cards issued in this era mainly because it was issued in the greatest quantities. Cards from this set are still relatively easy and inexpensive to find today, more than 75 years after their issue (Fig. 2-3).

Other Tobacco Sets

Many other tobacco sets were produced during these years, most of them issued by the American Tobacco Company. The company put out a gold-bordered set in 1911 (T205) and a brown-background set in 1912 (T207) that

Fig. 2-3. 1909–1911 American Tobacco Company cards (T206): Peaches Graham, George McQuillan, Ty Cobb, Tom Jones, Harry Howell.

Fig. 2-4. 1909–1915 era tobacco cards: 1912 American Tobacco (T207) Gabby Street, 1910 Obak (T212) Christian, 1912 Imperial Tobacco (C46) Ralph Stroud, 1911 American Tobacco (T205) Ed Karger, 1910 Old Mill (T210) Rose. Gabby Street once caught a ball thrown from the top of the Washington Monument.

featured mainly major league players. There were also tobacco sets that featured only minor league players. Sets issued with Contentnea, Old Mill, and Red Sun cigarettes featured Southern League players; Obak cigarette cards pictured players from the West Coast leagues; and a card set distributed by the Imperial Tobacco Company was issued in Canada, featuring players from the International League. Each of these sets contains from 75 to 500 different cards, and the cards are all small in size like the T206 cards (Fig. 2-4).

Though most of the cards issued in this time period are fairly standard in design and size, there are some sets that feature innovative designs. For example, the Ramly tobacco cards (1910) consist of black-and-white photographs with a very ornate design surrounding the pictures. The Hassan tobacco cards (1910) are three cards attached together and designed to be folded between the pictures. The Hassan cards contain a black-and-white action photograph in the middle and two small color portraits of players attached to either side. The

Fig. 2-5. 1909–1915 era candy cards: 1909–1911 American Caramel (E90-1) Cy Young, 1910 American Caramel (E91) Pat Donahue, 1910 Dockman (E92) Topsy Hartsel, 1911 E94 Patsy Dougherty, 1910 E98 Harry Davis.

Mecca tobacco cards (1910) feature two players sharing the same legs. The Mecca cards show one player when the top is folded up and another when it is folded down.

Most of the cigarette cards of this era were placed directly in packages of cigarettes, though some could only be obtained through mail-in offers. For example, cards from a set issued with Turkey Red cigarettes could only be secured by sending in a specified number of coupons found in the cigarette packages.

Candy Sets

There were many card sets issued with various candy products in the 1909–1915 era. These sets include the American Caramel set (E90-1) of 120 different major leaguers in full color, as well as various other sets containing between 25 and 50 cards. The candy cards from this era are usually similar to the tobacco cards, with many of the pictures coming directly from tobacco card sets. Candy cards from this era are generally much scarcer than tobacco cards and are often found in much poorer condition. The reason for this might be that the candy cards were collected more by kids and the tobacco cards more by adults, with the kids treating cards more roughly.

In 1914 and 1915, Cracker Jack issued cards as prizes with its candy. The Cracker Jack cards are larger (2¼″ × 3″) than most of the other cards of the time and feature a red background. These cards are very popular with collectors today. Interestingly, the entire 1915 Cracker Jack set of 176 cards could be obtained by mail in 1915 for one Cracker Jack coupon and 25 cents. The 1989 *Sports Collectors Digest Baseball Card Price Guide* values a complete set at $21,100.

In 1911, the Collins-McCarthy Company issued its first card set of West Coast minor league players. The cards were inserted with Zeenut candy, which was similar to Cracker Jack. Zeenut cards were issued for every year from 1911 to 1938, making their 28-year run the longest continuous streak of baseball card issues until 1979, when Topps passed this record. The end of the Zeenut issues came when the company went out of business.

Other Sets

Several other sets produced in the 1909–1915 era were issued with bread and consisted of 25 to 50 cards each. Another set contains over 280 cards that could be ordered by mail from *Sporting Life* magazine. A few other sets were issued with other sports magazines. Several sets of baseball cards were printed on materials other than cardboard, including leather, silk, and felt. There were also sets of cards that were issued in a small round style by gum and candy makers. More than 50 different baseball card sets were issued during these years, containing from 25 to over 500 cards.

1916–1931: Quiet Years

There were occasional issues of baseball cards from 1916 through 1931, including some fairly notable sets, but in general this period was very quiet. In retrospect, it seems rather strange that this would be a quiet period, since the country was in strong financial shape and Babe Ruth was making baseball more popular than ever before. The tobacco card sets were disappearing during these years, and they haven't returned since. Most of the cards issued during this era were either put out by candy companies or were issued in strips that could be cut apart (with no accompanying product).

Candy Cards

The most comprehensive card sets of this time period were the two large sets issued by the American Caramel Company in the early 1920s. The first set (known as E120) pictured 240 players (15 for each team), while the second set (known as E121) was issued in consecutive years, with the first set containing 80 cards and the second containing 120 cards. There are many variations found in E121, and the exact number of different cards available is uncertain. At 2″ × 3¼″ to 2″ × 3½″, these cards are larger than the majority of the cards that had been issued previously. They are generally not very popular with collectors, probably because they are black-and-white cards, with the E120s having a yellowish or a bluish tone. There were many other sets issued in this era that can be directly linked to these two issues because of the use of the same pictures and similar designs.

There were a few other candy sets issued in this era. A set issued by York Caramels in 1927 consists of 60 small black-and-white cards, and pictures from that set were used in several other sets from the same time period. Zeenut cards continued to be issued in all years of this era.

Strip Cards

In the 1920s, there were many sets of cards that were delivered to stores in uncut strips. The cards were designed to be cut apart by either the store owners or by the people who purchased them. Strip cards are usually crude color drawings of players printed on thin cardboard or thick paper. They have never been very popular with card collectors, and their values are usually fairly low. Most strip card sets contain between 30 and 120 cards with no advertising and no writing on the back. Almost all of the strip card sets were issued between 1920 and 1928 (Fig. 2-6).

1932–1941: Gum Cards

From 1932 through 1941 there were many major issues of cards, most by gum companies. Cards from this era vary in size and design, though most are larger than the early tobacco cards. The leading manufacturer of cards at the beginning of this era was the Goudey Gum Company, which issued six major sets from 1933 to 1941. Gum, Inc., which later became the Bowman Gum Company, was the leader at the end of this era, issuing major sets under the title Play Ball in 1939, 1940, and 1941. Many other gum companies produced card sets during this era as gum became the predominant product to be associated with baseball cards.

Fig. 2-6. *1916–1931 era baseball cards: 1920 Zeenut Worth, 1922 American Caramel (E120) Stanley Coveleskie, 1919 strip card (W514) Slim Sallee, 1928 strip card (W513) Eddie Roush, 1927 York Caramel (E210) Stanley Harris.*

Goudey

In 1933, Goudey produced its first baseball card issue of 240 full-color cards. These cards were a huge success and are still fairly plentiful today. Goudey followed up this first set with a new set of 96 cards in 1934 that featured comments about the players by Lou Gehrig and Chuck Klein, two prominent players of the era. In 1935, Goudey issued a set of cards with each card containing four small pictures of different players from the same team. The backs were designed as pieces of a puzzle. Goudey issued new sets in 1936, 1938, and 1941, with decreasing success. The company's later sets are more difficult to find today, probably because of lower sales at the time of issue.

Play Ball

The Play Ball sets of 1939, 1940, and 1941 that were issued by Gum, Inc., were very successful at the time and would probably have continued had World War II not come along. Play Ball sets contained 162 black-and-white cards in 1939, 240 black-and-white cards in 1940, and 72 color cards in 1941. Cards from all three

of these sets are plentiful today, with the 1941 set being the most expensive and sought after because of its use of color. In addition to these three main sets, Gum, Inc., also produced a sepia-toned card set in 1941, featuring two players per card.

Other Gum Cards

Many other gum card sets were issued in this era, including a set of 32 cards by the George C. Miller Company in 1933 (now very scarce), a set of 60 small cards by Tatoo Orbit in 1933, the Diamond Stars set of 108 cards issued by National Chicle from 1934 to 1938, and the Delong set of 24 cards issued in 1933. All of these sets are in color (Fig. 2-7).

Other Card Sets

There were some nongum sets distributed during these years, including Exhibit cards, the 1932 U.S. Caramel set, and the 1934 Rice Stix set. Exhibit cards were distributed from 1939 through 1966 by the Exhibit Supply Co. of Chicago. They are large ($3\frac{3}{8}'' \times 5\frac{3}{8}''$), thick, black-and-white or sepia-toned cards which

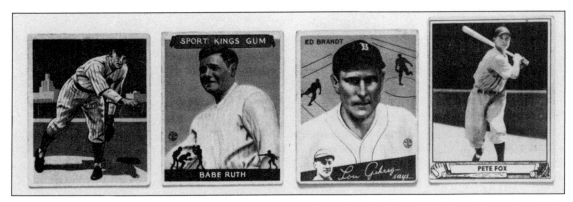

Fig. 2-7. 1932–1941 era gum cards: 1934–1936 Diamond Stars Tom Bridges, 1933 Sport Kings Gum Babe Ruth, 1934 Goudey Ed Brandt, 1940 Play Ball Pete Fox.

were generally sold in arcade vending machines for a penny. Exhibit cards are not very popular with collectors today. The 1932 U.S. Caramel set was a last attempt by the caramel companies to issue a baseball card set. This set did not have very good distribution at the time and is very scarce today. There was an offer on the backs of these cards for a free baseball or fielder's glove for sending in complete sets of cards to the company. For many years card number 16 was thought not to exist, possibly to save the company from having to give out any prizes. Recently, a card number 16 of Charles (Lindy) Lindstrom was discovered. The 1934 Rice Stix set consisted of just two cards (Dizzy and Paul Dean) given out with the purchase of shirts in the St. Louis area.

1942–1947: Quiet Years

From 1942 through 1947 there were very few card sets issued, and none of major importance. World War II effectively interrupted the release of baseball cards from 1942 through 1945, and it wasn't until 1948 that cards began to really appear again. There were some regionally issued baseball cards during these years, including cards of West Coast minor league players produced by Remar Bread starting in 1946 and continuing through 1950. There were other cards issued with bread in 1947, including a 13-card Jackie Robinson set issued by Bond Bread and a set of over 160 cards by Tip Top Bread.

1948–1955: The Modern Era Begins

In 1948, the Bowman Gum Company (formerly Gum, Inc.) ushered in the modern era in baseball card collecting by issuing a 48-card set of black-and-white cards. Bowman would continue to issue new card sets every year through 1955. Another gum company, Leaf, also issued a set of cards in 1948. The numbering in the 1948 Leaf set is very strange, for many numbers were never issued and many more were issued only in limited quantities. In 1951, Topps produced its first baseball card sets, and the company and its cards have been going strong ever since. Many other smaller card sets were issued during these years, some nationally and many others as regional sets for a particular team or area.

Fig. 2-8. Bowman baseball cards: 1948 Johnny Mize, 1950 Virgil Stallcup, 1951 Bobby Thomson, 1954 Alex Kellner.

Bowman

Bowman issued a small 48-card baseball card set in 1948, then released a new set of 240 cards in 1949. Bowman continued to release sets of between 224 and 324 cards every year through 1955 until the company was bought out by Topps. From 1951 through 1955 Bowman competed directly with Topps for the baseball card market. Both companies sought to obtain exclusive contracts of players for their sets. Because of this, many players can be found in either the Bowman or the Topps sets in these years, but not in both. For example, Stan Musial appeared in the Bowman sets of 1952 and 1953, and did not appear in a Topps set until 1958. Musial may have been missing from both the Bowman and Topps sets of the mid-1950s because of his affiliation with the Rawlings Sporting Goods Company, which issued cards of Musial in the mid-1950s to promote its sports equipment. The Bowman sets of the late 1940s and early 1950s really helped shape the modern baseball card collecting hobby, and most Bowman cards are plentiful today (Fig. 2-8).

Topps

In 1951 Topps Chewing Gum entered the baseball card market with five small sets of cards. The company followed these sets up with a bang in 1952 by issuing a 407-card set. The 1952 set was the largest set of cards issued in over 40 years, since the T206 set of 1909–1911. Topps continued to issue new sets every year. The Topps sets from 1953 through 1955 all contained over 200 cards, but none approached in size the 407-card set of 1952 (Fig. 2-9).

Other Card Sets

Many other baseball card sets were issued in the early 1950s. The immense popularity of the Topps and Bowman cards caused other companies to issue cards with their products. Cards were issued with many products that had never been associated with cards before. They were issued with cookies, breakfast cereal, hot dogs, potato chips, statues, and even dog food. They were issued with tobacco products for the first time since the 1909–1915 era

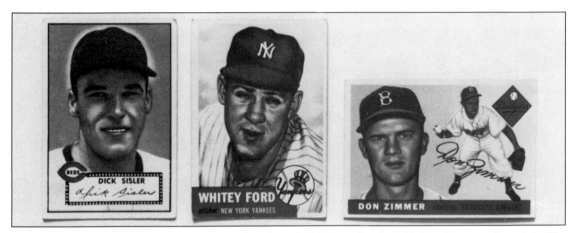

Fig. 2-9. Early 1950s Topps cards: 1952 Dick Sisler, 1953 Whitey Ford, 1955 Don Zimmer. Copyright The Topps Company, Inc.

Fig. 2-10. Cards from nonmajor issues of the 1950s: 1954 Johnston Cookies Johnny Logan, 1952 Wheaties Cereal Phil Rizzuto, 1954 Red Heart Dog Food Nelson Fox, 1954 Wilson Wieners Carl Erskine.

when Red Man Chewing Tobacco issued sets from 1952 through 1955.

Some of the sets that were issued included the Drakes Cookies set of 1950, the Mother's Cookies sets of 1952 and 1953, the Johnston Cookies sets of 1953 through 1955, the Wheaties Cereal sets of 1951 and 1952, the Wilson Wieners set of 1953, the Stahl Meyer meats sets of 1954 and 1955, the Hunters Weiners sets of 1953 through 1955, the Glendale Meats set of 1953–1954, the Esskay Meats sets of 1954 and 1955, the Briggs Franks set of 1953–1954, the Dan-Dee potato chips set of 1954, the Num Num potato chips sets of 1950 and 1952, the Robert F. Gould set of cards issued with statues in 1954, and the Red Heart

Fig. 2-11. Topps cards from the 1956–1980 era: 1959 Chuck Tanner, 1965 Ron Santo, 1967 Mets Maulers, 1978 Jim Palmer. Copyright The Topps Company, Inc.

Dog Food set of 1954. Each of these sets contained less than 100 cards, and most were only distributed in a particular region of the country (Fig. 2-10).

1956–1980: Topps Dominance

Topps

When Topps bought out Bowman between the 1955 and 1956 baseball seasons, Topps obtained a monopoly in issuing baseball cards with gum. From 1956 through 1980, Topps controlled the baseball card market by attempting to sign every major league player to an exclusive contract stating that the player's picture could not be placed on cards issued with gum from any other company. The strategy worked as well as Topps could have hoped, since it was the only company to issue major baseball card sets over this time period. Other gum companies such as Fleer and Leaf issued some small sets, but their cards had to be issued with other products or had to picture non-active players. Manufacturers of other products were still free to issue cards, and many small sets continued to appear. Topps began supplying baseball card sets to other compa-

nies to market with their products during these years, something Topps continues to do today.

The Topps sets from 1956 through 1980 are all large sets, and the number of cards in the sets generally stayed the same or grew larger from year to year. All of the Topps sets issued after 1958 contain over 500 cards, and the 1972 set contains 787 cards, making it the largest set of this time period. In 1957 Topps reduced the physical size of its cards to $2\frac{1}{2}'' \times 3\frac{1}{2}''$, and it has kept this size for every card issue from 1957 through the present, except for some cards that were issued in a smaller size in 1975 in addition to the regular-size set (Fig. 2-11).

From 1952 through 1973, Topps distributed its cards in different series throughout the summer. The company would usually put out the first 100 or so cards in April, then release the next 100 cards in May, and continue this for four to seven series. Because of this distribution pattern, cards from certain number groups are sometimes harder to find than other cards from the same set. In most cases cards in the last series are the toughest to find, since cards were not as widely distributed at the end of the baseball season. In 1974 Topps began distributing its entire set at one time, and this practice eliminated the scarcity of high-num-

Fig. 2-12. Cards from the 1956–1980 era: 1962 Post Cereal Don Drysdale, 1979 Hostess Reggie Jackson, 1960 Leaf Bill Virdon.

bered cards. Topps has been distributing cards in this manner ever since.

In addition to its regular sets, Topps issued many other sets during these years, some as inserts with regular issues and some as entirely separate issues. For example, Topps placed many card, poster, and coin inserts in its card packages from 1964 through 1971. Also, Topps produced small sets of larger-sized cards and sold them as separate products in 1964, 1970, 1971, and 1980.

The dominance that Topps enjoyed for 25 years came to an end between the 1980 and 1981 baseball seasons when the Fleer Corporation won a lawsuit with Topps stating that Fleer could issue baseball cards with its gum.

Other Sets

Even though Topps dominated the major set market during this era, there were a lot of smaller sets issued. Some of the smaller sets would have even been considered large sets in an earlier era.

Post Cereal issued 200-card sets in 1961, 1962, and 1963 that could be cut off the backs of cereal packages. The same cards were also printed on the back of Jello boxes in 1963 in a slightly smaller size. The cards were blank-backed, and many variations and scarcities have appeared, probably as a result of the cards being placed on the backs of different types of cereal. Cards that appeared only on the less popular types of cereal and Jello packages are generally more difficult to find today. For example, cards appeared on both 3-ounce and 6-ounce Jello boxes. Since collectors probably preferred the 3-ounce boxes, so they could get two cards for every 6 ounces of Jello they consumed, the cards appearing on the 6-ounce boxes are now generally harder to find.

Hostess issued 150-card sets from 1975 through 1979 that could be cut off the backs of boxes of snack cakes. The cards were produced by Topps for Hostess. These cards were the first cutout cards to feature statistics on the back. Like the Post Cereal cards, scarcities have developed for cards issued with only certain types of cakes (Fig. 2-12).

Kellogg issued 3-D cards in packages of cereal from 1970 through 1983. Complete sets of these cards could also be ordered through the mail in most years. The sets ranged in size from 54 to 75 cards. These cards are very colorful with informative write-ups on the back,

Fig. 2-13. Fleer cards from the 1956–1980 era: 1959 Ted Williams, 1963 Jimmy Piersall, 1971 World Series set (1918 World Series), 1975 Pioneers of Baseball Ed Delahanty.

along with complete statistics. A negative aspect of these cards is that they tend to curl because of the plastic used for the 3-D effect.

Kahn's Weiners issued card sets from 1955 through 1969. These sets consisted mainly of players from Midwest teams, usually the Cincinnati Reds, as Kahn's products were marketed in that area. Salada Tea produced sets of baseball coins in 1962 and 1963. Salada's 1962 set consisted of over 200 plastic coins with paper inserts of the players. There were 63 metal coins in the 1963 issue. Many other companies issued sets during these years, including Hires Root Beer in 1958, Leaf Gum in 1960 (the cards came with marbles), Bazooka Gum in most years from 1959 through 1971 (Bazooka is a Topps product), Milk Duds candy in 1971, and Burger King restaurants in the late 1970s.

Fleer

The Fleer Corporation, a gum manufacturer, attempted to get a foothold in the 1956–1980 era by issuing many small and unusual sets. Fleer issued an 80-card set in 1959 covering the life of Ted Williams, whom the company had signed to an exclusive contract.

In 1960 and 1961 Fleer issued cards featuring all-time great players, since these players were not under contract by Topps.

In 1963 Fleer attempted to issue a large set of current players that would rival the Topps set of that year. The cards were issued with cookies, since Topps had an exclusive contract to issue cards with gum. Fleer issued a first series of 66 cards with obvious plans to issue more series later in the year. For whatever reasons, Fleer did not issue any more cards that year.

In the late 1960s and early 1970s, Fleer issued a number of small, unusual baseball card sets. The company released an 18-card black-and-white set of cards featuring major league stadiums in 1969. In 1970 and 1971 Fleer issued cards featuring all of the World Series matches of the past, with each card bearing a cartoon on the front and a write-up on the back. In 1973 Fleer issued a set of cards entitled "Baseball's Famous Feats," featuring a cartoon on the card front and a write-up on the back focusing on some famous baseball feat, such as "Wahoo Sam Crawford Hit 312 Triples" or "Walter Johnson Won 38 1-to-0 games." In 1974 Fleer followed with a similar set called

Fig. 2-14. National major issue cards from the 1980s: 1983 Topps Jeff Reardon, 1989 Donruss Gregg Jefferies, 1989 Score Cal Ripken, Jr., 1981 Fleer George Brett. Topps card copyright The Topps Company, Inc.

"Baseball's Wildest Days and Plays," again featuring cartoons on the front. The company issued an interesting 28-card set called "Pioneers of Baseball" in 1975. These cards featured photographs of players from the early days of baseball, most of whom began their careers in the nineteenth century. At least two of the photographs used in the set were taken directly from Old Judge Cigarette cards that had originally been issued in the late 1880s. In 1976 Fleer went back to the cartoon format with a set called "Baseball Firsts" (Fig. 2-13). Fleer did not produce another baseball card set until 1981, after a court decision allowed them to produce a major set in direct competition with Topps.

1981–1990: Baseball Card Wars

Fleer had been trying to issue a baseball card set of current players for many years and was finally able to issue a major set in 1981 after winning a court decision that said that Topps was acting as a monopoly by not allowing other companies to issue baseball cards with gum. This ruling meant that other companies would be allowed to compete in the baseball card market. The ruling against Topps was not limited to Fleer only. Another gum company, Donruss, announced plans to issue a set in 1981.

The year 1981 was a boom year for baseball card issues. Topps, Fleer, and Donruss each issued sets of more than 600 cards. In addition, many smaller sets were issued. It was apparent to all that the years of the Topps monopoly on baseball cards had come to an end. Topps, Fleer, and Donruss continued to be the only companies producing major baseball card sets every year until 1986, when the SportFlics set appeared. The 1986 SportFlics set consists of 200 "Magic Motion" baseball cards that are produced by a company called Optigraphics. SportFlics cards each contain three pictures on the front, with different photographs appearing as the card is tilted. The SportFlics cards were sold with smaller "Magic Motion" trivia cards. SportFlics cards have continued to appear every year since 1986. In 1988, Optigraphics also put out the first edition of Score cards, a direct rival to Topps, Fleer, and Donruss. The first Score set contained 660 cards featuring color photographs on the backs of the cards as well as on the fronts (Fig. 2-14).

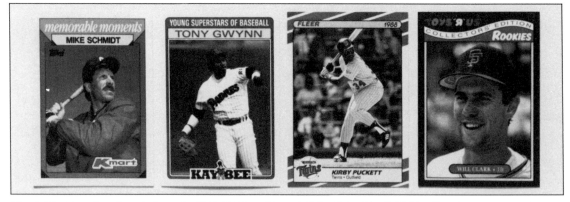

Fig. 2-15. Boxed set baseball cards: 1988 K-Mart (Topps) Mike Schmidt, 1986 Kay Bee (Topps) Tony Gwynn, 1988 McCrory (Fleer) Kirby Puckett, 1987 Toys 'Я' Us (Topps) Will Clark. Topps cards copyright The Topps Company, Inc.

Still another company, Upper Deck, produced its first major baseball card set in 1989. The first set contained 700 cards, with color photographs on the fronts and backs. The most unique feature of Upper Deck cards is that they also contain a small hologram of the company name on the back. The hologram was included as a deterrent to counterfeiters, along the same lines as the holograms that now appear on many credit cards.

A tremendous number of baseball card sets were issued in the 1980s. During the years of Topps dominance, there were usually only a few sets put out in a typical year in addition to the Topps set. During the 1980s, the number of sets issued in a typical year was usually over 100.

New Types of Cards

Many new types of baseball card sets were developed during the 1980s, including boxed sets, police sets, ballpark sets, and traded sets. Special edition sets also began appearing, featuring some or all of the reguar issue cards printed on a different size or stock of cardboard or on some other material. Small boxed sets of 33 to 44 cards featuring only star players

and sold as a complete set exclusively at one chain of stores began appearing with the issue of the 1982 K-Mart boxed set produced by Topps. In 1987 there were over a dozen of these boxed sets issued, all produced by Fleer or Topps (Fig. 2-15).

The first police baseball card set was issued in 1979 by the San Francisco Police Department. It featured cards of Giants players and was available from police officers and at a ballpark giveaway game. Many other baseball card sets sponsored by police and fire departments have been issued since, with some teams creating a new set annually. The Braves, Dodgers, and Brewers issued sets in most years from 1981 through 1989. The Blue Jays, Royals, Mariners, Phillies, Astros, Padres, Angels, and the minor league Columbus Clippers all issued at least one police or fire set in the 1980s (Fig. 2-16).

Baseball card sets available only at major league stadiums on specific card giveaway days became common during the 1980s. Many of the police sets were distributed in this way, as were sets sponsored by stores or corporations. Beginning in 1983, Mother's Cookies sponsored many baseball card giveaways at the

Fig. 2-16. Police cards: 1983 Dodgers Greg Brock, 1983 Brewers Robin Yount, 1981 Mariners Maury Wills, 1981 Braves Gene Garber.

Fig. 2-17. Baseball cards given out at ballparks: 1986 Mother's Cookies Astros Nolan Ryan, 1984 7-Up Cubs Lee Smith, 1983 Affiliated Food Stores Rangers Pete O'Brien, 1985 Mother's Cookies A's Dave Collins.

stadiums of teams in the western United States. The Cubs and the Indians have had an annual baseball card giveaway game every year starting in 1982, and the White Sox and the Rangers have had one every year starting in 1983. All of these teams have changed sponsors for their sets at least once, but the sets have continued. In 1987 there was a perforated sheet of large baseball cards given out at almost every ballpark, with a sheet featuring a star from every National League team given out at National League stadiums and a sheet of American Leaguers given out at American League parks (Fig. 2-17).

In 1981 Topps issued a set of baseball cards late in the baseball season called the "Traded" set, featuring players who had changed teams or rookies who had not appeared in their regular set. This set was not available to the general public in traditional ways but was available only through baseball card dealers. Topps has continued to issue new Traded sets every

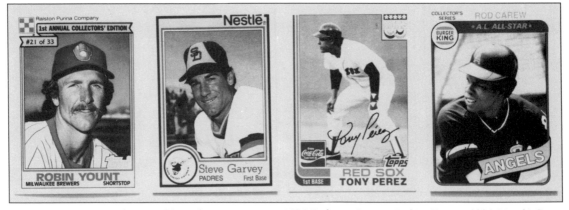

Fig. 2-18. Topps cards issued by other companies: 1984 Ralston Purina Robin Yount, 1984 Nestlé Steve Garvey, 1982 Coca-Cola/Brigham's Tony Perez, 1980 Burger King Pitch, Hit & Run Rod Carew. Copyright The Topps Company, Inc.

year since. In 1984 Fleer began issuing its own late-season set, calling it the "Update" set and distributing it in the same way as the Topps Traded set was distributed. Fleer has continued issuing these sets every year since. In 1985 Donruss began issuing a "Highlights" set featuring highlights of the previous baseball season and issued a late-season "Rookies" set in 1986. These cards were also distributed only by baseball card dealers and have continued to be issued since.

Because of the great demand for baseball cards, the major card manufacturers began issuing special varieties of their regular cards. In 1984 Topps issued a set of 30 cards that were identical to regular Topps cards of superstar players except that the cards in the special set were much larger and had different numbers on the backs. Topps also issued a specially boxed edition of its entire 1984 set using white cardboard with a glossy finish and called it a "Tiffany" set. The Tiffany set was sold only through baseball card dealers, as a complete set. At about this same time Topps began making small metal versions of a few of its regular cards, and these too were available

only through baseball card dealers. Topps has continued to produce these types of sets.

In 1987 Fleer issued a "Tin Glossy" set that was similar to the Topps Tiffany sets. The cards were identical to the Fleer regular issue except that they were printed with a high-gloss finish and were housed in a special tin box. Complete sets were available from baseball card dealers only. The Tin Glossy set has continued to be produced since 1987.

In 1985 Donruss issued a set that was identical to the "Diamond Kings" subset of the regular Donruss issue except that the cards were larger in size. These cards were available through a write-in offer on the wax wrappers of Donruss regular baseball cards. Donruss has continued to produce these sets every year.

Other Cards

In addition to the major issues and the new types of cards, cards continued to be offered with other products in the 1980s. Many of these sets were produced by Topps or by Michael Schechter Associates (MSA) for other companies, while some were produced by the individual companies themselves.

Fig. 2-19. MSA cards issued by other companies: 1984 Stuart Expos Gary Carter, 1987 Jiffy Pop Roger Clemens, 1986 KAS Cardinals Jack Clark, 1986 Meadow Gold milk Dwight Gooden.

Topps produced the following sets for other companies: Drakes Cake sets found on the East Coast from 1981 through 1988, Gardner's Bread Brewers from 1983 through 1985, Nestlé chocolate bars in 1984 and 1987, Wendy's Restaurant Tigers in 1985, many Coca-Cola sets from 1981 and 1982, Hostess Cakes Braves in 1985, and some others (Fig. 2-18).

MSA produced the following sets for other companies: discs found in potato chips in 1986 including Kitty Clover Royals, KAS Cardinals, and Jays (Brewers, Cubs, White Sox); Jiffy Pop discs from 1986 to 1988; Kraft Macaroni cards in 1987; M&M's cards in 1987; various Meadow Gold milk and ice cream cards in 1986; Bohemian Hearth Bread Padres cards in 1987; Fantastic Sam's haircut cards in 1988; and others. Most of the MSA sets are easy to recognize because the team insignias on the hats of the players have been airbrushed off because MSA was not licensed by the teams to show insignias for these sets (Fig. 2-19).

Other sets produced in these years include the Granny Goose potato chips A's cards from 1981 through 1983, the Nalley's potato chips Mariners set of 1983, a set of all-time greats issued by Big League Chew Gum in 1986, and 7-11 Slurpee Coin sets produced from 1983 through 1986.

Rare and Valuable Cards

There are some very rare baseball cards in existence, and these cards are usually very valuable. Rarity is not the only criterion for value in baseball cards, however. The most valuable baseball card in existence is the T206 card of Honus Wagner, which is listed at $95,000 in top condition in the 1989 *Sports Collectors Digest Baseball Card Price Guide*. The Wagner card is very rare, but there are other baseball cards that exist in smaller quantities and are worth far less money.

Table 2-1 presents some of the most highly valued cards, with prices taken from the 1989 *Sports Collectors Digest Baseball Card Price Guide*. The prices listed are for cards in near-mint condition. There are other cards that have

Table 2-1. Some High-Value Cards and Their 1989 Values

Card Set	Player	Value ($)
T206	Honus Wagner	$95,000
1933 Goudey	#106 Lajoie	15,000
T206	Plank	9,000
T206	Magie	8,000
1952 Topps	#311 Mantle	6,500
1951 Topps All-Stars	Konstanty, Roberts, Stanky	5,500 (each)
1933 Goudey	Ruth	2,800–3,300*
T207	Lowdermilk, Lewis, Miller	2,800 (each)
E90-1	Mitchell (Cincinnati)	2,200
1954 Bowman	#66 Williams	2,000
1953 Glendale Meat	Houtteman	1,900
N28	Anson	1,000
1963 Topps	#537 Rose	575
1984 Donruss	#248 Mattingly	65

*There are four different 1933 Goudey Ruth cards, thus the price range.

values higher than some of the cards listed in Table 2-1, but those listed are a good representation of some of the more valuable baseball cards. There are specific reasons, discussed below, why all of the cards on this list are more valuable than the average baseball card.

The T206 Honus Wagner Card

The most valuable baseball card in existence today is the T206 card of Honus Wagner. It was once thought that there were only a handful of these cards, but it is now speculated that there are anywhere from 40 to 80 copies in existence. Frank Barning stated in a 1987 issue of *Baseball Hobby News* that he has seen 25 different specimens and has heard of others.

The T206 Wagner is definitely not the rarest baseball card. One of the reasons for its value comes from the fact that it is a rare card that belongs in one of the most popular base-ball card sets of all time. Another reason for its value is that it has received much publicity over the years as the most valuable baseball card. The most famous early baseball card collector, Jefferson Burdick, had a lot of trouble locating this card and may have started it on its way to fame by publicizing its scarceness. (Burdick finally did obtain a copy of this card as a gift from a collector friend.)

Most collectors have heard that this card is rare today because Wagner was a non-smoker and objected to the use of his picture for the purpose of selling cigarettes. This was just a well-known, handed-down rumor for many years until Bob Lemke of *Sports Collectors Digest* published a story in 1986 that told of a 1912 article in *The Sporting News* that confirmed—and had probably been the ancient foundation for—the rumor. A passage from the October 24, 1912, issue of *The Sporting News* reads as follows:

Not long ago a firm of tobacco manufacturers wrote to a local newspaper man, and asked him to secure a picture of Hans Wagner to be given away with cigarets, together with the written permission of the big Dutchman to use it. The writer was promised a liberal fee for his work in lending the photo.

The scribe wrote to Wagner, and asked him for the picture enclosing the tobacco company's letter. A few days later he received a communication from Hans, saying that he did not care to have his picture in a package of cigarets, neither did he wish his friend to lose the chance to cop a little extra coin. "So," he concluded, "I enclose my check for the amount promised you by the tobacco company, in case you got my picture, and hope you will excuse me if I refuse."

The newspaper man sent the check back, with a higher opinion of Wagner than he had ever possessed before, though the two had always been close friends.

This passage confirms the fact that Wagner objected to the use of his picture as an advertisement for cigarettes. It does not note that the card was actually produced. It may be that the card was designed and issued before The American Tobacco Company was aware of Wagner's objections. A small quantity of the cards were issued before the card was pulled from distribution. A threat of legal action by Wagner or simply the concern of that possibility by American Tobacco is likely to have led to an end to its distribution and to its scarcity today.

Honus Wagner was a great shortstop from 1897 through 1917, mostly with the Pittsburgh Pirates. He compiled a lifetime batting average of .329 and was among the first five players to be inducted into the Hall of Fame. He was elected in 1936 along with Ty Cobb, Babe Ruth, Walter Johnson, and Christy Mathewson. Because of his stature as one of the all-time greats of baseball, Wagner's card is all the more valuable. It is almost mind-boggling that the value of the T206 Wagner card in near-mint condition is listed at $95,000, while the second most valuable card in the guides doesn't even reach $20,000.

The 1933 Goudey Napoleon Lajoie Card

The 1933 Goudey card of Napoleon Lajoie is valued at $15,000. This card was never actually issued with the 1933 Goudey set, but instead was printed in 1934. In the 1933 set, Goudey issued cards with numbers from 1 to 240, except that it did not issue a card for number 106. Collectors of the time complained to the company that they could not complete their sets without a card number 106. Because of the complaints, Goudey created the Napolean Lajoie card number 106 in 1934. The card is unique in that it contains the back design of a 1933 Goudey card and a front design that is similar to a 1934 Goudey (Fig. 2-20).

Only a small number of these cards are in existence today. The card may never have been available to the general public, even in 1934. Jefferson Burdick received a small quantity of the Lajoie card directly from Goudey in 1934 and gave them to fellow collectors. This may have been the only way it was distributed, but in a 1973 issue of *The Sport Hobbyist*, writer Lionel Carter speculated that the card may also have been distributed in very small quantities with 1934 Goudey cards. He reported that collector Buck Barker remembered getting one with bubble gum, and that recently another Lajoie card had been found in a collection of

Fig. 2-20. 1933 Goudey Napoleon Lajoie.

1930s cards that was unlikely to have come from Burdick. Interestingly, an uncut sheet of 1934 Goudey cards that contains the Lajoie card is in existence.

Adding to the value of this card is the fact that Nap Lajoie was a great second baseman from 1896 through 1916, compiling a lifetime batting average of .339. He was inducted into the Hall of Fame in 1937, the second year of elections.

It is worth mentioning that this is one of the few *valuable* baseball cards picturing a player who was retired at the time of issue. There have been many baseball card sets issued that have depicted baseball greats after they retired; however, very few cards from these sets have become valuable, even though the players pictured are all greats of the game. Baseball card collectors generally prefer cards of players that are active when the cards are issued.

T206 Plank

The Plank card is another very rare and valuable card in the T206 set, although not nearly as valuable as the T206 Wagner. Rumor has it that the T206 Plank is rare because the printing plate for this card was damaged early in the print run of T206 cards and was not repaired or replaced. Though there is some evidence to dispute this rumor, no other speculations have been made for its scarceness. Eddie Plank is in the Hall of Fame as a pitcher, compiling 327 wins in a career that went from 1901 through 1917, and this adds to the value of the card.

T206 Magie

The T206 Magie card is rare because the card was changed to correct an error in the spelling of the player's name. This card depicts Sherry Magee, an outfielder for the Phillies. When the card was first issued, Magee's name was misspelled Magie. The card was corrected soon after, creating two variations of the card. The error version is valued at $8,000, while the correct version, a fairly common card in the T206 set, is valued at $65 (Fig. 2-21).

1952 Topps Mantle

The 1952 Topps card of Mickey Mantle (#311) was issued as one of the high-numbered cards of the set. The high-numbered 1952 cards (311–407) are considerably more rare than the other cards from this set because of limited distribution. Even the least valuable cards among these numbers are valued at $150. This card was the first that Topps made of Mickey Mantle, and Mantle cards are among the most popular in the baseball card hobby. Interestingly, the high-numbered cards of Mantle, Jackie Robinson, and Bobby Thomson were double-printed, meaning that twice as many cards were printed for these players as for any other player in the high-numbered series.

1951 Topps Current All-Stars

In 1951, Topps produced five small sets of baseball cards, including a set of 11 current All-Stars. Cards for Konstanty, Roberts, and

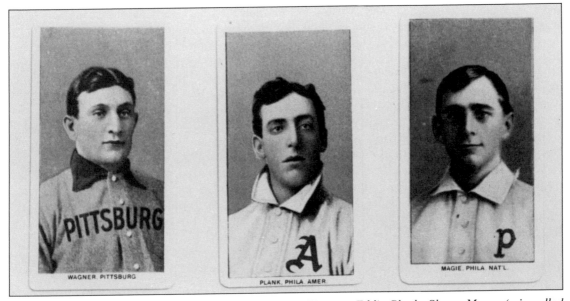

Fig. 2-21. Three rare and valuable T206 cards: Honus Wagner, Eddie Plank, Sherry Magee (misspelled Magie).

Stanky were printed but were never sold to the general public with the others in the set. Only a few of these cards are known today. These cards are valued at $5,500 each, while the other eight cards that were issued to the general public are valued at between $175 and $650 each.

1933 Goudey Ruth

There are 240 cards in the 1933 Goudey Gum set and four separate cards picture Babe Ruth. There are also two cards of Lou Gehrig. Ruth and Gehrig were the biggest names in baseball when this set was issued, so multiple cards were made of them. Every other player in the set was pictured on only one card. The Ruth and Gehrig cards are valued from $1,800 to $3,300, while common cards from this set are listed at $45. The price difference is solely because of the star quality of the players. The cards themselves are no rarer than any others in the set. In fact, the Ruth card #144 was the

only card in the set that was double-printed, making it twice as common as any other card in the set. The Ruth card #144 is listed at $2,800.

Babe Ruth is considered by many to be the greatest player of all time. He was the dominant player of his era, leading the American League in home runs 12 times. He retired after the 1935 season with 714 home runs, and this remained the highest home run total for any player until 1974, when Hank Aaron broke his record. Ruth also compiled a lifetime batting average of .342 and was walked over 2,000 times, the most of any player in the history of the game. Baseball cards of Babe Ruth are always worth more than cards of other players in the same set.

T207 Lowdermilk, Lewis, Miller

The T207 set of 200 players was distributed by the American Tobacco Company in 1912. The cards all contain brown backgrounds and feature mostly obscure players. There are many scarce cards in this set, mainly due to the fact that the cards were sold with several different brands of cigars and cigarettes and not all of the cards were issued with each brand. The rarest of the cards in this set feature Louis Lowdermilk, Irving Lewis, and Ward Miller. It is unknown exactly why these three cards are rarer than the other rare cards in the set. None of these three was a particularly good player, so the value of the cards derives only from their scarceness.

The Irving Lewis card is not only rare, but it also can be found in two variations, one showing a Braves patch on Lewis's arm and the other showing no patch. Interestingly, Irving Lewis never played in a major league game.

E90-1 Mitchell

The E90-1 set was distributed by the American Caramel Company in the 1910 era. It is probably the most popular of the early candy sets. There are 120 different cards, with some of the cards rarer than others. The rarest card in the set is that of Mike Mitchell of Cincinnati. (There is another Mitchell in the set, Fred Mitchell of New York.) It is speculated that part of the reason that the Mitchell card is scarce is that it was not distributed with the set until very late in the promotion. Though there are other rare cards in this set, the Mitchell card is listed at almost three times the value of the next rarest card in the set ($2,200 as compared to $800).

1954 Bowman #66 Williams

Contractual problems probably led to the scarcity of 1954 Bowman Ted Williams cards. This card was pulled from distribution and replaced with a card of Jim Piersall. Both Williams and Piersall cards display the number 66. In the early 1950s there was a lot of compe-

tition between Topps and Bowman to get players signed to exclusive baseball card contracts. Topps was probably able to get an exclusive on Williams, forcing Bowman to withdraw its Williams card. In the 1954 Topps set, Williams is the only player to be pictured on two different cards. The distribution of the 1954 Bowman Ted Williams card is unknown, but it may have been very strange. Well-known card collector Larry Fritsch once reported that he never saw a Williams card until late in the year, when he opened a pack of cards and found eight Williams cards out of the ten cards in the pack. A friend of Fritsch reportedly found six in another pack. The 1954 Bowman Ted Williams card is extremely scarce, and its value is increased because it pictures Hall of Famer Williams.

1953 Glendale Meats Houtteman

The 1953 Glendale Meats card of Art Houtteman is the rarest card in a scarce regional set of Detroit Tiger cards issued in the Detroit area. The Houtteman card is valued at $1,900, while common cards from this set are listed at $90 each. Houtteman's card was probably pulled from distribution early in the promotion because the Tigers traded him to Cleveland in June of 1953; thus, the card is extremely scarce.

There have been other cards that have been pulled out of their sets early or altered because of player trades. This almost always causes the original card to go up in value, as the pulled card is automatically more difficult to find than other cards in the set. A recent example of this happening was with the 1981 Granny Goose card of Dave Revering. All of the other cards of common players in that set are listed at $2, while the Revering card is listed at $45 because it was pulled when Revering was traded.

N28 Anson

Cap Anson was the finest player of the nineteenth century and was baseball's first true superstar. Anson's career began in 1871 in the first year of the National Association, the first professional baseball league. He played through all five years of that league's existence, then joined the National League in its inaugural year of 1876 as a member of the Chicago Cubs. He played for Chicago from 1876 through 1897, compiling a .334 lifetime average and becoming the first player to ever get 3,000 hits. In Anson's day, 3,000 hits was an even more difficult feat than it is today because the number of games played in a season was much lower than it is now. Through his first eight years in the National League, Anson played in an average of 73 games a season. By contrast, baseball seasons now consist of 162 games. In addition to being the finest player of the nineteenth century, Cap Anson was also the manager of the Chicago Cubs from 1879 through 1898. The Cubs won five pennants during Anson's years as manager. Anson was elected to the Hall of Fame in 1939.

Baseball cards of the nineteenth century that picture Cap Anson are worth far more than cards of lesser players. The N28 cigarette card of Anson that was issued in 1887 is listed at $1,000, while cards of common players are listed at $175. The N28 card of Anson is no rarer than the other cards in the set, but Anson's presence makes it much more valuable. As another example of Anson's appeal, N172 cards depicting Anson are listed at $750, while common players are listed at only $65.

1963 Topps Rose

The 1963 Topps card of Pete Rose (#537) was one of the first cards to have its value greatly increased by the fact that it was the rookie card of a star player. Until the early

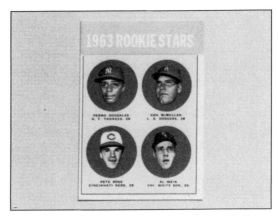

Fig. 2-22. 1963 Topps Pete Rose rookie card. Copyright The Topps Company, Inc.

1980s there was little or no value added to anybody's rookie card. It is unknown how the rookie craze got started, but the rookie cards of prominent players are now listed at many times the value of later cards featuring the same player. The 1963 Topps Rose card is listed at $575, while his 1964 Topps card is valued at $150 and most of the Topps Rose cards from the 1970s are listed at less than $20 (Fig. 2-22).

Aside from the fact that the 1963 card was Rose's first appearance on a Topps card, the card also was issued in the last series that year. Cards from the last two series in 1963 are much scarcer than cards from other series. Common cards from the last series are valued at $4, while lower-numbered cards from the set are listed at 70 cents.

1984 Donruss Mattingly

The 1984 Donruss card of Don Mattingly (#248) is listed at $65 and is on this list of valuable baseball cards because of some new factors that have influenced its value. The 1984 Donruss Mattingly card was the first card of a relatively young player that passed the $50 mark based mostly on his potential of becoming an all-time great player. Recently, Jose Canseco's 1986 Donruss card made a similar climb. When Mattingly had three straight great years from 1984 through 1986, winning the batting title in 1984 and the MVP award in 1985, baseball card collectors and investors took notice. The value of 1984 Topps and Fleer Mattingly cards rose over the $10 level, and the 1984 Donruss Mattingly skyrocketed to well over $50.

The reason the Donruss card of Mattingly rose so much more than the Topps or Fleer cards of him is because the 1984 Donruss set is much scarcer than either the 1984 Topps set or the 1984 Fleer set. In 1984, Donruss cut down on its production of baseball cards because of overproduction from 1981 through 1983. Collectors who had grown accustomed to waiting until the end of the year to get Donruss cards cheaply were caught unprepared when there were no new Donruss cards available in late 1984. They then began scrambling for the available cards, driving up the price of 1984 Donruss cards. Prices have remained high for 1984 Donruss cards, with the Mattingly card being the most sought-after card in the set.

While the values for the other cards on this list of valuable cards will probably remain high over the years, the 1984 Donruss card of Mattingly is not yet established as a long-term valuable card. The performance of Mattingly will determine the final value of this card. While Mattingly has had a great career to date, he is a long way from the Hall of Fame. The Hall of Fame is one of the best guarantees of long-term value for a player's baseball cards. Mattingly won't qualify for induction into the Hall of Fame until after the 1992 season, since a player must play for 10 years before being eligible. A lot can happen between now and the end of Mattingly's career. It is always possible that a current player's performance may drop to lower levels in future years or that the player may get injured or even die. Baseball history is full of players who began their careers with some great years and never made it into the Hall of Fame. Herb Score is a prime example of a player who had a great start in the majors, followed by an injury that ended his career well before its time. Score led the American League in strikeouts and won 36 games during his first two years in the majors in 1955 and 1956 before he was hit in the head with a line drive early in the 1957 season. Though he came back to pitch for several more years, he never regained his early greatness. Thurman Munson may never make it to the Hall of Fame because of the years of his career that were lost when he died tragically in a plane crash. On the other hand, if a current player does make it to the Hall of Fame, cards depicting that player should go up in value.

Baseball Card Manufacturers

Early Baseball Card Manufacturers

It is unknown who had the original idea to produce a set of baseball cards. There was one man who was instrumental in issuing trading cards with his products in the early years of baseball and that man was Buck Duke.

James Buchanan Duke and the American Tobacco Company

One of the main issuers of baseball cards, both in the 1887–1890 years and again in the 1909–1915 era, was a man by the name of James Buchanan ("Buck") Duke. Duke is probably best known today through Duke University in Durham, which was named after him because of his generous contributions to the school. Duke issued baseball cards and cards of other subjects as inserts with his cigarettes. He issued cards under the W. Duke Sons & Company name in the 1887–1890 years and under various cigarette names such as Piedmont, Sweet Caporal, Old Mill, and others in the 1909–1915 years (T205, T206, T207, etc.). All these brands of cigarettes were produced by the American Tobacco Company, which was run by Duke (Fig. 3-1).

Duke was a self-made millionaire cigarette producer. He introduced many innovations into the cigarette industry and was the first manufacturer to use machine packaging of cigarettes. Duke greatly believed in advertising, and his company advertised more heavily than any other cigarette company of its time.

In the 1880s, Buck Duke was one of the partners in a small tobacco company named W. Duke Sons & Company. He was the son of Washington Duke, who started the company as a means of selling the tobacco he grew on his farm. At this time there were many tobacco companies that were larger than Washington Duke's, the largest of which included Allen & Ginter (producers of the N28, N29, and N43 baseball card sets), Kinney Tobacco Company, Kimball (N184), and Goodwin & Company (N172). These were considered the big four tobacco companies of the time, and they produced most of the baseball cards and other card sets that were issued in the late 1880s.

Buck Duke's goal was to become the superpower of the tobacco industry, just as John

Fig. 3-1. James Buchanan Duke. (Photo courtesy of Duke University Archives.)

cards into his cigarette packages in the late 1880s. It is unclear whether his was the first company to insert cards into cigarette packages, but it was certainly one of the first. The cards that were inserted into cigarette packages in the 1880s became an instant hit, and most of the large cigarette manufacturers began issuing their own card sets to keep up with the competition. The pictures came in numbered sets, and kids began pestering their dads for them. Soon collecting cards became a craze, and the demand for cards forced the tobacco store owners of the time to carry the cigarettes in large quantities (Fig. 3-2).

By 1889 W. Duke Sons & Company was the largest cigarette manufacturer in the United States. In the year 1889, Duke produced 940 million of the 2.1 billion cigarettes that were consumed in the United States. He was soundly beating his competition, but he was just getting started. In 1890 Duke convinced the other four major cigarette manufacturers to join forces with him and form the American Tobacco Company, with himself installed as president. With a virtual monopoly on the cigarette industry, the American Tobacco Company began eliminating the expenses that were associated with competition. Prices for cigarettes were raised, advertising budgets were lowered, prizes and kickbacks for retail store owners were stopped, and baseball cards and other card sets were eliminated from cigarette packages. The main reason that baseball cards virtually disappeared from tobacco products from 1890 to 1908 was because the American Tobacco Company was in place as a virtual monopoly in the tobacco industry and did not need cards to stimulate sales.

Under Duke's direction, the American Tobacco Company continued to grow, branching out into other forms of tobacco products such as cut plug (chewing) tobacco. In the late 1800s, chewing tobacco was more popular than cigarettes, though cigarettes were gaining rap-

D. Rockefeller had become the superpower of the oil industry. In the 1880s, Duke began using machines to produce cigarettes and thus gained a big jump on his competition. Using machines made it possible to make just about as many cigarettes as he could sell, so he began a heavy advertising campaign to reach as many cigarette consumers as possible. He began giving away prizes and kickbacks to store owners that sold his cigarette products. He would send his own people around to tobacco stores to ask for his cigarettes by name.

Duke would do just about anything to sell his cigarettes. He began inserting collecting

Fig. 3-2. Tobacco cards issued by W. Duke Sons & Company and the American Tobacco Company: 1880s Duke's Cameo Actresses (N145) Violet Cameron, 1889 Duke's Actors and Actresses (N71) Maurice Barrymore, 1909–1911 American Tobacco (T206) Dode Criss, 1911 American Tobacco (T205) Sam Leever, 1909 American Tobacco Flags of All Nations (T59) Sweden.

idly in popularity due to the American Tobacco Company. In 1898 Duke formed the Continental Tobacco Company by joining together most of the leading cut plug tobacco companies, including P. H. Mayo & Brother (N300).

Over the next decade, Duke continued to branch out. He formed the American Cigar Company to try to capture part of the cigar market in the United States. He worked increasingly hard on exporting his tobacco products to foreign countries, and he set up plants in some of these countries to cut costs and to get around import restrictions. He also helped set up a chain of retail tobacco outlets to handle his tobacco products and used his power to drive most of the small private tobacco shops of the time out of business. The huge conglomeration that was put into place by Duke was becoming known as the "tobacco trust."

One of the many cigarette companies that was bought out by Duke was the R. J. Reynolds Tobacco Company, which joined the Continental Tobacco Company in 1899. The owner of this company, Dick Reynolds, hated the tobacco trust and Buck Duke, but Reynolds sold his company to avoid being run out of business by the giant conglomerate. One of the stipulations of his sale to the trust was that he remain in charge of his business. During the years that the R. J. Reynolds Tobacco Company was owned by the tobacco trust, Duke always gave Reynolds a free hand in running his company. Reynolds himself was always independent-minded and hated being subservient to the trust.

Over the years the huge tobacco empire that Duke had built up had been generating a great deal of resentment from the American public. Tobacco farmers were being paid a lower rate for their tobacco, since there was very little free market activity any more; independent retail tobacco stores and tobacco companies were being run out of business; and other similar large monopolies were being attacked and split up by the United States government. In response to this growing wave of criticism, Duke began to conceal his new acquisitions in a complex network of corporations that were all owned by American Tobacco. Many of the new companies that were acquired continued to operate in the same manner as before and kept their original company names and product names. It was not made public knowledge that they were subsidiaries of American Tobacco; in fact, some of these companies were instructed to openly pretend that they were independent.

In 1907, President Theodore Roosevelt and the U.S. government sued to dissolve the tobacco trust. It took four years of trials before a decision was reached by the U.S. Supreme Court to dissolve the trust. After months of trying to untangle the corporate maze and work out a plan to break up the monopoly, the government decided that the only man who could do the job was Duke himself. Ironically, Duke was given the task of breaking up the monopoly he created. As in most things he did, Duke did a brilliant job of it, and much of today's tobacco industry is still run according to his organizational decisions of that time.

It was during the years that the tobacco trust was engaging in its intense legal battles for its very existence that baseball cards began to appear once again in cigarette packages. From 1909 to 1911, the most famous baseball card set from the early part of the century was issued, the T206 set. It ushered in a new era of tobacco card sets that were produced on a scale unlike anything seen since the 1887–1890 years. From 1909 to 1915 there were numerous baseball card sets and other types of card sets issued. Some of the most well-known sets from this time are all of the *American Card Catalog*–numbered sets from T200 to T217 and the T3 Turkey Reds set. In addition to the tobacco cards issued in this era, cards began appearing with many other types of products, including candy, bread, and sports publications (Fig. 3-3).

It is obvious from the backs of tobacco cards of this era that there was a tobacco trust in force in the United States. The T206 set alone was issued with 16 different brands of

Fig. 3-3. Piedmont cigarette package from the 1910 era. Piedmont was a popular cigarette brand made by the American Tobacco Company. Baseball cards from sets such as T206 were found in packages like this.

cigarette advertisements on the card backs, with no mention of the American Tobacco Company. Most of the other cigarette card sets of this era can be found with more than one brand of cigarette advertisement on the back. The T216 Kotton Cigarette set of cards issued by the People's Tobacco Company even goes so far as to state on the card backs that the company is not part of a tobacco trust.

In late 1911, Duke proposed a plan to split up the tobacco trust into four separate companies, with each of the new presidents hand-picked by Duke. One of these four companies was to be the R. J. Reynolds Company, with ownership returning to its original owners. The U.S. Government approved Duke's plan, much to the joy of Dick Reynolds. One of the provisions of Duke's new organization of the tobacco industry was that the top executives of the four new companies would each receive 10 percent of the net profits of their companies. Duke instituted this arrangement to give the executives a greater incentive to earn higher profits. Duke retained a large chunk of stock in each company, and since he no longer held control, he wanted to be sure the new owners had an incentive to increase their earnings. His

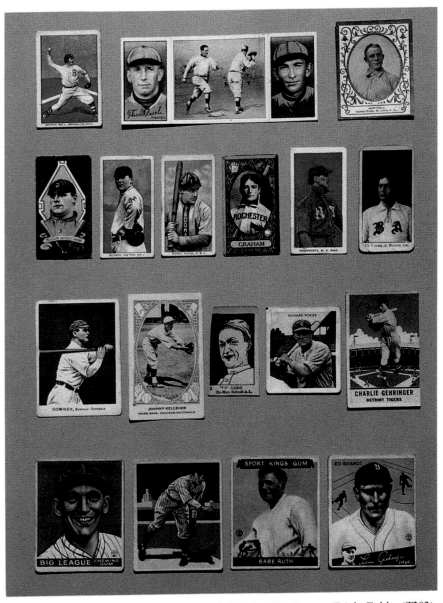

Row 1: *1911 Brunners Butter Krust Bread (D304), 1912 Hassan Triple Folder (T202), 1909 Ramly Cigarettes (T204).* *Row 2:* *1911 American Tobacco Co. Gold Border (T205), 1909–1911 American Tobacco Co. White Border (T206), 1912 Obak Cigarettes (T212), 1912 Imperial Tobacco Co. (C46), 1911 E94 candy card, 1909–1911 American Caramel Co. (E90-1).* *Row 3:* *1915 Cracker Jack (E145-2), 1922 American Caramel Co. (E120), 1926 Strip Card (W512), 1933 Tatoo Orbit gum, 1933 DeLong Gum Co.* *Row 4:* *1933 Goudey, 1934–1936 Diamond Stars, 1933 Sport Kings (Goudey), 1934 Goudey.*

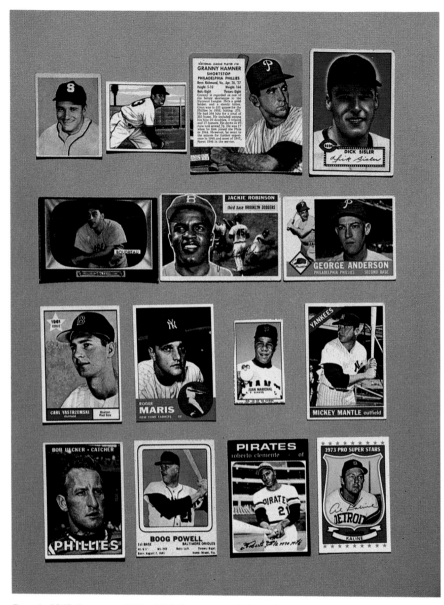

Row 1: 1949 Bowman PCL, 1950 Bowman, 1953 Red Man Tobacco, 1952 Topps. Row 2: 1955 Bowman, 1956 Topps, 1960 Topps. Row 3: 1961 Topps, 1963 Topps, 1966 Bazooka, 1966 Topps. Row 4: 1967 Topps, 1970 Transogram, 1971 Topps, 1973 Kellogg.

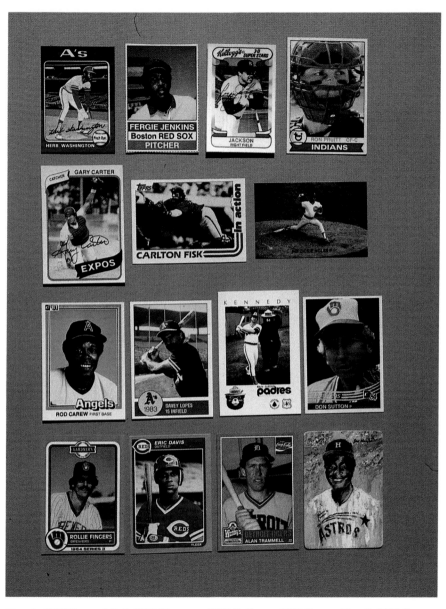

Row 1: 1975 Topps Mini, 1976 Hostess, 1978 Kellogg, 1976 Topps. *Row 2:* 1980 Topps, 1982 Topps, 1983 Thorn Apple Valley Cubs. *Row 3:* 1981 Donruss, 1983 Granny Goose, 1984 Smokey the Bear Padres, 1984 Donruss. *Row 4:* 1984 Gardners Brewers, 1985 Fleer, 1985 Wendy's Tigers, 1986 Mother's Astros.

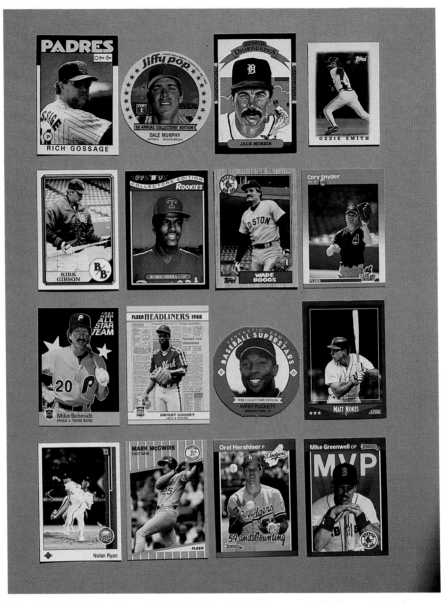

Row 1: 1986 O-Pee-Chee, 1986 Jiffy Pop, 1987 Donruss, 1988 Topps Mini League Leaders. *Row 2:* 1987 Boardwalk and Baseball, 1987 Topps Toys 'Я' Us, 1987 Topps, 1987 Fleer. *Row 3:* 1987 Fleer All-Star, 1988 Fleer Headliners, 1988 Fantastic Sam's, 1988 Score. *Row 4:* 1989 Upper Deck, 1989 Fleer, 1989 Donruss, 1989 Donruss MVP.

Fig. 3-4. The message on the back of the Camel Cigarettes package has remained the same since 1913.

plan worked brilliantly, and in a few years each of the four new companies was returning greater profits than the entire trust had returned prior to its dissolvement.

The company that became the leader in the new tobacco industry was the R. J. Reynolds Company. In 1913, Reynolds introduced Camel cigarettes, which became hugely successful. On the back of each package was printed this message:

Don't look for premiums or coupons, as the cost of the tobaccos blended in CAMEL Cigarettes prohibits the use of them.

This message effectively ended the use of baseball cards and other premiums as inserts in packages of cigarettes. The message was a brilliant ploy for increasing tobacco sales, but it was terrible for card collectors. It hinted that the use of cards and other premiums was bring-

ing down the quality of the cigarettes. Since none of the other tobacco manufacturers wanted their products to be known as low-quality cigarettes, every tobacco manufacturer soon abandoned cards as a means of increasing sales.

The message on the back of Camel cigarette packages was so effective that within three years there were no baseball cards being given away with cigarettes, and there have never been any cigarette baseball cards since (in over 70 years). Interestingly, the message is still being displayed on the back of packages of Camel cigarettes as this book is being written in 1990 (Fig. 3-4).

The American Caramel Company

In the years following the American Tobacco Company's reign as the top issuer of baseball cards, there was no rush by other companies to carry on the tradition. Most of

Fig. 3-5. American Caramel Company baseball cards: 1922 E120 Bill Wambsganss, 1922 E121 Johnny Mostil, 1927 E126 Lu Blue. Wambsganss executed the only unassisted triple play in World Series history in the 1920 World Series.

the baseball card sets issued over the next 20 years were produced by companies as one-time promotions.

Probably the most important baseball card manufacturer that immediately followed American Tobacco was the American Caramel Company. Incorporated in 1898, the American Caramel Company of Pennsylvania issued its first set of baseball cards with its caramel candy in 1908. The company issued other baseball card sets in various years through the late 1920s. In addition to baseball cards, it also created trading card sets featuring many other subjects, including navy ships, flags, prizefighters, movie actors and actresses, and the wild west.

The first baseball cards issued by American Caramel came out at about the same time American Tobacco was issuing its cards, around 1908 to 1909. American Caramel issued two full-color sets, each with the small size of the tobacco cards. American Caramel's E90-1 set is one of the most popular early candy sets, while its E91 set is probably the least popular. The E91 cards are known for their "fake designs," meaning that the pictures on the cards often do not resemble the player identified in the caption.

American Caramel released a new set of cards in 1915 featuring pictures of players that had previously been used in earlier sets. In the early 1920s it released two large sets of new cards, known as E120 and E121. These were the most comprehensive sets of the 1920s. The E120 set pictured 240 players, 15 from each team. The E121 set was issued in two consecutive years, with 80 cards issued in the first year and 120 in the second. Many of the pictures were repeated for the two years, and many variations are known. The pictures used in the E120 and E121 sets were used in several other sets of the 1920s that were produced by various manufacturers (Fig. 3-5).

Fig. 3-6. Goudey cards through the years: 1933 John Schulte, 1935 (Mickey Cochrane, Charlie Gehringer, Tom Bridges, Billy Rogell), 1938 Rudy York, 1941 Bill Posedel.

American Caramel issued a final, very obscure, baseball card set of 60 players in 1927. Although it issued no more baseball cards after 1927, the company did issue a set of American Historical Characters cards in the early 1930s before bidding farewell to the card business.

Goudey Gum Company

The baseball card giant of the early 1930s was the Goudey Gum Company of Boston. Goudey issued six major baseball card sets between 1933 and 1941, as well as several other minor sets. In addition to baseball cards, Goudey also issued cards of other subjects, such as Indians, jungle scenes, action scenes, boy scouts, and the history of aviation.

Goudey's 1933 baseball card set is among the most popular sets of all time. The company issued 240 full-color cards that year, and they were a huge success. Goudey began the practice of issuing its cards in different series, with different groups of the 1933 set available at different times throughout the summer and into the fall. The last group of 1933 cards was issued so late in the year that some of the write-ups on the card backs even contain references to the 1933 World Series.

Goudey followed with another successful set in 1934, this one containing 96 cards. Though the 1934 cards were again very popular with collectors, the drastic decrease in the number of cards in the set was not a good sign. It indicated that Goudey's commitment to baseball cards was not as high as might have been expected from the industry leader (Fig. 3-6).

Goudey's new sets issued in 1935 and 1936 met with decreasing success, because the quality of the cards was deteriorating with each set. The 1936 set consisted of black-and-white cards, a further indication of Goudey's lack of commitment to quality. The company didn't even put out a new set in 1937. Goudey came back with a very innovative color set in 1938, with each card containing a photograph of a player's head attached to a cartoon body. After waiting three years, Goudey put out its final set in 1941, an unsuccessful issue of very poor quality cards. At the time of Goudey's last card issue, the company had clearly lost its number one position to Gum, Inc., which would later be known as Bowman Gum, Inc. Goudey went out of business in 1962.

Bowman Gum, Inc.

The leading baseball card company in the late 1930s and 1940s was Bowman Gum, Inc.

In the 1930s a man named Warren Bowman ran the company. He hired an advertising man named George Moll to help sell his Blony bubble gum. Moll was a collector of British cigarette cards and wanted to use trading cards to help sell the gum. Many other bubble gum companies had already used trading cards with great success. The company released a hugely successful card set named "Horrors of War" in the late 1930s, shortly before World War II began. The set was featured in a two-page article in *Life* magazine, and many of the cards contained grotesque drawings of war scenes. Three of the cards in the set feature Adolph Hitler, and these are very highly valued today. Shortly after this war set was issued, the company put out its first set of baseball cards.

The company was known as Gum, Inc., when it released baseball sets titled "Play Ball" in 1939, 1940, and 1941. Each of these sets was well-received by collectors of the time. The first two sets were in black-and-white, while the third was in color. Plans for a 1942 set were scrapped when the United States entered World War II in late 1941.

It was not until 1948 that the company would release its next baseball card set, this time using the Bowman name. The 1948 set featured 48 black-and-white cards and ushered in the modern era of card collecting. Bowman released a new set of 240 color cards in 1949 and continued issuing large sets of baseball cards every year through 1955.

In addition to the baseball cards, Bowman also released many other sets of trading cards. The subjects of these sets included Mickey Mouse, the Lone Ranger, movie stars, and many war-related issues.

Bowman's 1948 set of baseball cards encountered some competition when Leaf, Inc., issued a set of baseball cards that year. Bowman and Leaf had some legal squabbles, and Leaf soon abandoned the baseball card field after that one set. A new competitor named Topps would not be beaten so easily. After Topps issued its first sets of baseball cards in 1951, Bowman took the company to court to try to stop it from issuing more cards. Bowman's lawsuit was unsuccessful, and Topps continued to issue baseball cards in direct competition with Bowman in the early 1950s. Topps proved to be the winner of the struggle for baseball card supremacy when it bought out Bowman after the 1955 baseball season.

The Current Card Companies

The majority of baseball cards being issued these days are produced by six companies: Topps, Fleer, Leaf (Donruss), Score/SportFlics, Upper Deck, and Michael Schechter Associates (MSA). In order to produce a set of current major league baseball player cards these days, companies have to obtain certain permissions first.

Permissions Required for Putting Out a Baseball Card Set

All of the current card companies have received permission from the Major League Baseball Players Association (MLBPA) to picture current major league players on baseball cards. In addition, all of them except MSA have permission from Major League Baseball (the major league team owners) to display official major league baseball team logos and insignias on their cards.

Major League Baseball Players Association (MLBPA)

The MLBPA is the baseball players union. You hear about this organization most often when it's time to negotiate another labor agreement between players and owners every few years. In addition to handling labor agreements, the MLBPA also handles endorsement agreements for major league players as a group. By signing an agreement with the MLBPA, baseball card companies can acquire the right to picture any current major league player on their cards.

It is much easier for a card company to negotiate one contract with the MLBPA than to negotiate individually with the players. Fleer and Donruss contracted with the MLBPA in 1981 and have renewed their contracts every year since. The Score, SportFlics, and Upper Deck sets all have MLBPA approval. MSA contracted with the MLBPA for its baseball disc sets in 1976 and for many of the other sets it has issued over the years.

Topps was the last major baseball card company to sign a contract with the MLBPA, which didn't happen until 1987. Since the early 1950s, Topps had signed individual contracts with all of the players appearing in their sets. Since virtually every major league player was already signed to a Topps contract, Topps didn't think an agreement with the MLBPA was necessary. During the 1980s, the MLBPA did not like the fact that Topps did not use the MLBPA's services in obtaining player contracts. The

MLBPA felt that Topps was trying to restrict fair competition by using individual contracts. In the mid-1980s, the MLBPA began advising all players not to sign contracts with Topps until Topps signed an MLBPA agreement. Several players followed this advice and did not sign with Topps, most notably Kevin McReynolds. This put some pressure on Topps and caused Topps to eventually sign an MLBPA agreement in 1987.

Major League Baseball

The second permission that most baseball card producers obtain is from the major league team owners. The team owners control the right to display team logos and insignias. Topps, Fleer, Donruss, Score/SportFlics, and Upper Deck are all licensed by Major League Baseball. MSA is not.

MSA has never been licensed by Major League Baseball. Apparently the company doesn't consider team logos to be an essential element in its card sets. In most of MSA's sets, the team emblem is airbrushed off the caps of the players. MSA uses head shots of the players almost exclusively, so it doesn't have to make the effort to airbrush the team uniforms. MSA has used team logos on occasion. For example, in the 1987 Bohemian Bread Padres set the Padres logos are not airbrushed away. MSA probably avoided Major League Baseball by signing an agreement directly with the Padres for the use of the team's logos in that particular set.

Major League Baseball licensing is not automatic for manufacturers willing to pay the required royalties. Companies wishing to become licensed must submit a product idea when applying for the license and be willing to pay an 8½ percent royalty, with all licenses requiring an annual guarantee concerning royalties. After this application process a decision is made by Major League Baseball as to whether or not to grant the manufacturer a license.

Topps

Topps Chewing Gum, Inc., was established in 1938 by four Shorin brothers: Abram, Ira, Joseph, and Philip. Their original plan was to set up a company to produce chewing gum. They named the company Topps because of their goal to make the company tops in its field, with the extra *p* added for distinctive identity. The company's original chewing gum was priced at 1 cent each and was a popular changemaker on store counters throughout the country.

Topps began marketing its first bubble gum product in the late 1940s after World War II had ended. It was also in those years that Topps began inserting picture cards with its gum products. In 1948, Topps issued a set of 252 "Magic Photos" cards (Fig. 3-7). Nineteen of the photos pictured baseball players, making them the first Topps baseball cards. The card fronts were blank when taken from the pack, but then developed into black-and-white photographs when exposed to light.

In 1951, Topps produced its first sets of cards featuring only baseball subjects. The company issued five different sets that year, each containing from 9 to 52 cards. Topps has continued to issue baseball card sets every year since, and it has now issued sets in more consecutive years than any other company in history. Topps has also issued more than 25,000 different baseball cards, far more than any other card producer.

Competition with Bowman

When Topps began issuing baseball cards in 1951 it was not alone in the field. Bowman Gum, Inc., had been issuing baseball card sets since 1948, and had issued Play Ball baseball

Fig. 3-7. 1948 Topps Magic Photos Cy Young, Wire Haired Terrier. This set of various subjects comprised the very first Topps baseball cards. These cards are very small in size, at ⅞" × 1½". Copyright The Topps Company, Inc.

cards from 1939 to 1941 under the name Gum, Inc. When Topps began competing directly with Bowman, both companies tried to find a way to get an edge.

From 1948 through 1952, Bowman baseball cards were relatively small in size, a bit smaller than the standard cards of today. In 1952, Topps issued its cards in a large size, a bit larger than the cards of today. The larger cards issued by Topps were an attempt to impress the kids and get them to buy their cards. It is unknown whether the kids were impressed, but Bowman was. In 1953, Bowman issued its cards in a similar large size (Fig. 3-8).

In the early 1950s, both Topps and Bowman sought to obtain exclusive contracts from individual major league players to appear on their cards. As a result, neither company could issue cards of all of the stars of the day. In the mid-1950s, both Topps and Bowman had trouble filling out their sets with major league players. It got to the point that some of the cards even featured coaches and umpires, people who are rarely seen on baseball cards.

After the 1955 baseball card season, Topps bought out Bowman. The buyout of Bowman paved the way for a Topps monopoly on the baseball card business from 1956 through 1980. For this period, Topps was the only company that issued major baseball card sets.

Fig. 3-8. Topps and Bowman cards from the early 1950s: 1951 Topps Blue Back Bruce Edwards, 1952 Bowman Vic Wertz, 1955 Bowman Danny O'Connell. Topps card copyright The Topps Company, Inc.

Contract Issues

When Topps began issuing baseball cards in the 1950s, it had to get permission from the players. Topps did this by signing the players to individual contracts. When possible, the company signed players to exclusive contracts, prohibiting other gum makers from issuing cards depicting players with whom Topps had contracts.

After Topps eliminated its main competition by buying out Bowman, it set out to make sure nobody else would become as troublesome as Bowman had been. Topps was successful in signing just about every major league player to an exclusive contract. Then the company went even further, sending representatives to the minor leagues and signing contracts with everybody that it considered to be a major league prospect.

The terms of the player contracts were pretty favorable for Topps. Topps would give a minor league player a very small sum of money (as low as five dollars) for exclusive five-year rights to picture the player on Topps baseball cards if and when the player reached the majors. After the player reached the majors, he

would be paid a specific sum of money per year for the life of the contract. Topps would often renew the contracts for future years before they expired. The exclusive rights prohibited any other company from issuing baseball cards of the player with candy or gum products, or by themselves with no other product. Other baseball cards continued to appear with such items as cereal, meat products, soda pop, and other products that fell outside of the exclusive Topps agreement.

In the late 1950s and early 1960s, a couple of gum companies tried with limited success to break into the baseball card business. Fleer signed Ted Williams to an exclusive contract and issued a set of cards featuring him in 1959. Fleer then issued sets of retired great players in the early 1960s and began to issue a set of current player cards in 1963. Fleer tried to get around the exclusive Topps player contracts by issuing its 1963 cards with cookies, instead of gum. The cookies had to be made with a low sugar content because of the Topps contracts prohibiting anyone else from issuing cards with candy. At a court hearing in 1963, a Topps executive testified that the cookie tasted like

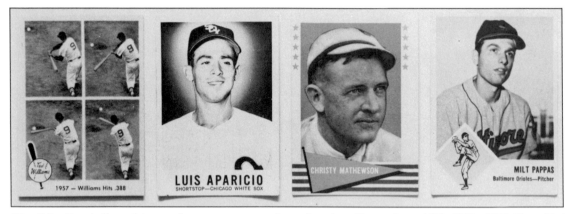

Fig. 3-9. Baseball card issues from gum companies other than Topps from 1959–1963: 1959 Fleer Ted Williams, 1960 Leaf Luis Aparicio, 1961 Fleer All-Time Greats Christy Mathewson, 1963 Fleer Milt Pappas.

"a dog biscuit." Perhaps because of public rejection of its cookies, Fleer issued only one series of what looked like a planned large set in 1963, and did not issue cards of current players again until 1981. Leaf, another gum company, issued a small set of current player cards in 1960 with marbles instead of gum. Leaf did not issue another set of baseball cards until after it merged with Donruss in the mid-1980s (Fig. 3-9).

Because of the stranglehold that Topps held over the competition, the Federal Trade Commission (FTC) filed a complaint against Topps in January of 1962, charging the company with monopolizing the baseball card business. Hearings were held over the next few years, generating a massive amount of documentation. Over 4,000 pages of transcribed testimony, 432 government exhibits, and 341 defense exhibits came out of the hearings. On May 21, 1965, the FTC ruled that the nearly exclusive major league baseball player contracts held by Topps did not give them illegal control of the market. Topps had won and now had an even firmer hold on the baseball card market.

Topps did have some problems with player contracts over the years. There were a few players who refused to sign. In 1958, one of the Topps scouts went to a minor league camp and signed every player except one to a Topps contract. The scout didn't sign the last player because he felt that there was no way that player could make it to the major leagues. That player was Maury Wills, who became a star in the early 1960s with the Los Angeles Dodgers. Wills even won the National League MVP award in 1962. Because the Topps scout had refused to sign him while he was in the minors, Wills held a grudge and would not sign a Topps contract. Wills came up to the majors in 1959 and did not make an appearance on a Topps baseball card until 1967, when he finally relented and signed. After the Wills fiasco, Topps began signing every minor league player to a contract, regardless of apparent ability (Fig. 3-10). Though Wills is the most notorious, there have been a few other players that have been missing from Topps baseball cards while still in their prime, probably due in most cases to low fee offers from Topps. Some other players who did not appear on Topps cards at times

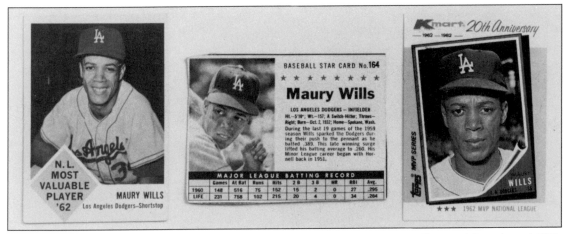

Fig. 3-10. Maury Wills baseball cards: 1963 Fleer, 1961 Post, 1982 K-Mart. Fleer and Post issued Wills cards in the early 1960s while Topps did not because of permission problems. This 1982 K-Mart card pictures Wills on a card with a 1962 Topps design, even though Wills did not appear in the 1962 Topps set.

during their careers include Rusty Staub, Tony Horton, and Chris Short in the 1960s and early 1970s.

In June of 1975, Topps faced a new challenge to its exclusive player contracts. The Fleer Corporation, an old enemy, filed a lawsuit accusing Topps of illegal restraint of trade. The lawsuit was also directed at the MLBPA, which was governing some of the terms of the Topps baseball contracts. On July 1, 1980, a federal judge ruled that Topps was guilty of violating antitrust laws and monopolizing the baseball card business. As a result of this ruling, Fleer was able to issue baseball cards with its bubble gum in 1981. Since the decision allowed others to compete in the baseball card market, Donruss also issued a baseball card set with gum in 1981.

Topps appealed the 1980 decision to a higher court, and on August 25, 1981, a three-judge panel of the United States Court of Appeals reversed the decision of the lower court, saying there was no illegal restraint of trade with the Topps contracts. Because of this rul-

ing, Fleer and Donruss could no longer issue baseball cards with gum. They also could not issue baseball cards alone without gum, as this was another area where Topps had exclusive contracts. Both Fleer and Donruss decided to continue to issue baseball cards with other products. Since 1982, Fleer has issued baseball cards with team logo stickers and Donruss has issued cards with puzzle pieces. Though these are thinly disguised gimmicks to get around the Topps contracts, both companies have successfully issued baseball cards every year since. When SportFlics and Score baseball cards began to appear in the late 1980s, they were issued with "Magic Motion" trivia cards (Fig. 3-11).

Topps continues today to try to sign every minor league player to exclusive contracts. Topps remains the only company that can issue baseball cards with gum or by themselves with no other product. Since 1981, when competition began with Fleer and Donruss, the Topps baseball card wrappers have stated that their baseball cards are "The Real One." It is

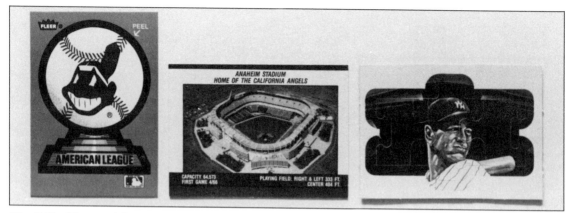

Fig. 3-11. Fleer and Donruss inserts: Fleer team logo sticker, the back of a Fleer sticker featuring major league stadiums, Donruss Lou Gehrig puzzle pieces.

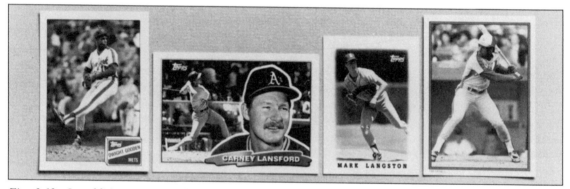

Fig. 3-12. In addition to its regular set, Topps also issued these other baseball card sets in 1988: 1988 Bazooka Dwight Gooden, 1988 Big Baseball Carney Lansford, 1988 Mini League Leaders Mark Langston, 1988 All-Star Glossy Tim Raines. Copyright The Topps Company, Inc.

interesting that with all of the intense efforts by Topps over the years to prohibit others from issuing baseball cards, sales of Topps products have skyrocketed since competition began.

Topps Minor Sets

In addition to major baseball card sets, Topps has issued many other types of cards over the years.

Separate Issues. In many years, Topps has issued other baseball card sets in addition to the major issue. Examples include the 1955 Dou-

ble Header cards; the Topps Giant cards of 1964, 1970, and 1971; the 1964 Stand-Ups; the Bazooka sets of 1959 to 1971; the Bonus Send-In Glossy sets of the 1980s; and sticker sets from various years. There have been few years when Topps was content to issue only its major set (Fig. 3-12).

Inserts. Topps has included special inserts with many of its card sets over the years. These include baseball coins in 1964 and 1971; bonus bucks in 1962; special small card sets in 1965, 1968, and 1969; posters in 1967 and 1970; and

Fig. 3-13. Topps inserts: 1988 Rookies (found only in Jumbo Packs) Mark McGwire, 1971 Coins Brooks Robinson, 1968 Game Willie Mays, 1970 Story Booklets Ernie Banks. Copyright The Topps Company, Inc.

Fig. 3-14. Topps nonbaseball cards: 1971 Football Joe Namath, 1963 Astronauts John Glenn, 1966 Batman, 1972 Presidents Richard Nixon (Nixon was still in office when this card was issued). Copyright The Topps Company, Inc.

glossy All-Star and glossy rookie cards in the 1980s. Topps has often been creative with inserts, and sets are highly collected (Fig. 3-13).

Test Issues. Topps puts out test issues of minor sets on occasion, often only in certain regions of the country. For example, Topps issued a set of baseball coins only in the New York area in 1987. The 1975 Topps Mini set was issued in only a few areas. Some Topps test sets are never issued at all, but still find their way into the baseball card collecting hobby.

The 1967 Topps Stand-Ups set is an example of a test set that was never issued. Since test sets see only limited or no distribution, they are rare and are highly valued.

Nonbaseball Issues. Topps does not deal exclusively with baseball when it comes to issuing card or sticker sets. Topps put out a football card set in 1950 and has been regularly issuing football card sets since 1955. Topps has issued many basketball and hockey sets over the years and has also issued sets featuring many nonsports subjects such as popular television shows ("Batman," "The Partridge Family," "Charlie's Angels"), movies (James Bond, *Star Wars*), and various other subjects (Man on the Moon, U.S. Presidents, The Beatles, Funny Valentines). In recent years, Topps issued the Garbage Pail Kids stickers. Topps has probably produced more U.S. nonbaseball card sets than any other company (Fig. 3-14).

Foreign Issues. Different versions of Topps baseball cards have been issued in other countries. For every year since 1965, the O-Pee-Chee Company of Canada has issued Canadian versions of Topps baseball cards. Cards from these sets are usually exactly the same as their U.S. counterparts except that they display the O-Pee-Chee name instead of Topps. Topps has also sold variations of its U.S. sets in some Latin American countries, most notably Venezuela. Most of the Venezuelan Topps cards found today were issued in the 1960s. Topps also issued a set of baseball cards in Great Britain for the first time in 1988. These cards featured American players, but were different from any U.S. issue.

Topps Licensing to Other Companies. In addition to creating its own card sets, Topps has also created cards for other companies on occasion. Topps produced the Hostess baseball cards of the late 1970s, Squirt cards in 1981 and 1982, Nestlé cards in 1984 and 1987, Gardner's Bread cards from 1983 to 1985, and various others.

Speculation on Quantities Printed Each Year

Topps does not announce how many baseball cards it produces each year, and none of the other baseball card manufacturers announce their numbers either. Collectors have always been eager to know this information so they can determine the relative scarcity of particular cards. Though exact figures are unavailable, estimated minimum amounts for recent years can be determined through information supplied by Topps giveaway bonuses and from Topps net sales figures.

In 1984, Topps included a special All-Star baseball game bonus card in each wax pack of baseball cards. These were used to give away various prizes. Listed on the card are odds of 1 in 2,700 for winning one of 20,000 pairs of batting gloves. Multiplying gives a figure of 54 million game cards, or 54 million wax packs. Each wax pack contained 15 cards in 1984, so multiplying further gives a figure of 810 million cards sold by wax pack in 1984. A similar game in 1985 wax packs indicates that 50 million wax packs were produced that year. Topps continued to include bonus contest cards in packs from 1986 to 1988, but no odds were given for any prizes, perhaps because the company realized that it was inadvertently giving away information about the quantities it was producing.

The 1984 Topps baseball card set contains 792 different cards. Based on 810 million cards sold, it seems apparent that Topps issued over 1 million copies of each card in the set. Remember also that these figures are based only on *wax pack* sales of baseball cards. Topps also issues cards in several other ways, most notably through rack packs and vendor cases that are sold directly to baseball card dealers. Adding cards sold in ways other than wax packs could easily boost the total number of each card issued to 1.5 million or more for 1984, and about the same for 1985.

In its annual report to stockholders in 1988, Topps listed sales figures for the last three years. In the year ended March 1, 1986 (the 1985 baseball card year), net sales of collectible picture products stood at over $39 million. Two years later, in the year ended February 27, 1988 (the 1987 baseball card year), net sales of collectible picture products were over $127 million.

Since their net sales more than tripled, it can be *speculated* that their card production also tripled. If you triple the speculated 1985 wax pack sales figures, this would put the number of 1987 Topps baseball cards produced at more than 2.4 billion, or 3 million of each card in the set. Clearly Topps is currently issuing a lot of baseball cards each year.

Distribution of Individual Cards in a Set

People have long been suspicious of baseball card companies. It seems that just about everyone has a story about how hard it was to get a certain card in a set. One person could never find a Mickey Mantle card, and another says that Mike Schmidt was next to impossible to get. In the Peanuts cartoon by Charles Schultz, reprinted at the beginning of this book, Charlie Brown could never get a card of his favorite player, Joe Shlabotnik. Some people have even suggested that card companies make it harder to get cards for certain teams in certain areas. The theory behind this speculation is that the card companies want customers to keep buying cards, so they make the most desirable cards the hardest to get.

The people from Topps have always maintained that equal numbers of each card are produced each year. In general, they are telling the truth. In most cases, if you can't get the card you want, it's just bad luck. There have, however, been some notable exceptions.

Cards Issued by Series. From 1952 through 1973, Topps issued cards in different series throughout the summer. This practice often led to cards from certain series being more difficult to find than cards from other series. In most of these years, cards from the last series are more difficult to find than cards issued earlier. When Topps was issuing cards in this way, it is unlikely that the company consciously tried to print smaller quantities of the high-numbered cards in order to create a scarcity. Rather, the

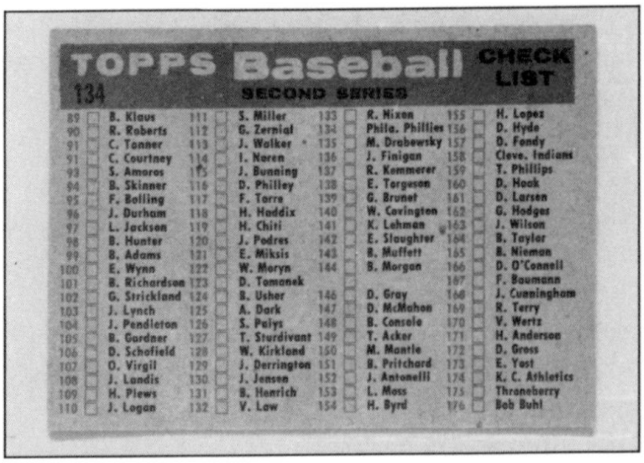

Fig. 3-15. This 1958 Topps checklist card shows no player listed for number 145. Number 145 was not issued that year. Copyright The Topps Company, Inc.

smaller printings of these cards was more the result of a lack of demand, since the baseball season was coming to an end when they were issued. *Within each series,* equal numbers of each card were generally issued.

Missing Numbers. In several sets of Topps cards, there were numbers that were skipped. For example, the 1953 set is missing six numbers and the 1955 set is lacking four numbers. In the 1958 set, there was no card number 145, though every other number was used from 1 to 495. In 1961, there were no cards for numbers 426, 587, and 588, with every other number used from 1 to 589. Card numbers 51 and 171 were never issued in the 1986 set (Fig. 3-15). In all of these cases, collectors would have had good reason to be suspicious of Topps. Skipping numbers in a set was a practice that was started with the 1933 Goudey set. Card number 106 was never issued that year, leading many outraged collectors to accuse Goudey of purposely trying to get collectors to buy more cards in the hopes of getting number 106 to complete their sets. Goudey did issue a number 106 card of Nap Lajoie in 1934, possibly because of some angry letters from collectors.

In fairness to Topps, in each case where a number was skipped in one of its sets, there is an explanation. For example, in 1953 and 1955, Topps had some contract problems and were unable to issue cards of some players at the last minute because the players were under exclusive contract to Bowman. In 1986, two cards were misnumbered, leaving two numbers picturing two players each, and two other numbers picturing nobody. Still, even though the company had an explanation for the missing numbers, most collectors never knew why the numbers were missing, and it would have been difficult to verify that the cards were missing at the time of issue in 1986.

Double-Printed Cards. Topps prints all of its cards in sheets, then cuts the individual cards from these sheets. In some years, there were two of some cards and one of others on a particular sheet. Two of the same card on a sheet is called double printing, and it causes some cards to be more abundant than others. It is usually done only when the number of cards in a set cannot be divided evenly into the number of cards that fit onto the sheets. For example, in recent years Topps has been printing 132 cards per sheet. From 1978 through 1981, Topps issued sets containing 726 cards. Since 132 doesn't divide evenly into 726, there were a number of cards that were double-printed during those years. From 1982 to the present Topps has been issuing sets of 792 cards, and since this number can be evenly divided by 132, there have been no double-printed cards.

Variations. Many players who have changed teams are pictured with their old teams when baseball cards are issued at the beginning of the year. This is because the cards are designed in the fall, before most player transactions are completed. The card companies also sometimes make mistakes on cards, such as picturing the wrong player, printing incorrect statistics, or making various other errors. When

Fig. 3-16. 1974 Topps San Diego and Washington variations for Willie McCovey. Copyright The Topps Company, Inc.

these things happen, the card companies usually don't do anything about it; however, occasionally a company decides to print a new version of a card during the year, and this creates a *variation*.

Whenever a variation is created, there are two different cards with the same number for a given set. All variation cards are scarcer than other cards in the same set, since the other cards were issued for the entire print run and the two variations were each issued for only part of the run. Sometimes one version of a variation is much scarcer than another, and sometimes the two versions are issued in approximately equal numbers. It's sometimes hard to tell during the year of issue which variation will be scarcer in the long run.

Probably the most notable variations created by Topps occurred in 1974, when they printed some of the San Diego Padres players with a team designation of "Washington Nat'l." At the time, there was a lot of speculation that the Padres would be moving to Washington D.C. for the 1974 season. Topps gambled and lost when it printed the Washington team designations. They corrected the team names soon after the initial release of cards, when it became apparent that the Padres wouldn't be moving. Today, the Washington versions of those variations are much scarcer than the San Diego versions (Fig. 3-16).

The Michigan, Ohio, and Indiana Test of 1984. For 1984, it is difficult to believe that Topps printed the same number of cards for each player in the set. This is because they tried an experiment that year in Michigan, Ohio, and Indiana. Some of the packages of baseball cards that were issued in those states offered collectors the opportunity to write to Topps and purchase any 10 different cards of their choice for $1.00 or 20 different cards for $1.00 plus 10 baseball card wrappers. The purpose of this experiment was supposedly to help collectors complete their sets. What probably happened instead was that a large number of collectors wrote in to request cards of superstar players. Because collectors almost certainly didn't request all of the players in equal numbers, Topps had several choices. It could pull the requested superstars from the existing stock of cards and sell the leftover unpopular cards in some packs (which would have been unfair to collectors buying packs), or it could throw away the leftovers (which would have been a waste of cards and revenue for Topps). Or, it could print up special sheets of cards with only the popular superstars on them (which would alter the usual distribution of equal numbers of each card).

It appears that Topps chose to print up the special sheets of cards with only the popular superstars. There is a known sheet of 1984 Topps cards containing multiple cards of many superstars. Included on the 132-card sheet are cards of only 50 different players, with 43 of the cards printed in multiples of two to five. There are five Darryl Strawberry cards on the sheet, with multiple cards of many other superstars such as Don Mattingly, Reggie Jackson, Pete Rose, Nolan Ryan, and Mike Schmidt. The quantity of these superstar sheets that were printed and distributed is not known, but it is clear that Topps printed more cards of some players than others during 1984.

The Future of Topps

Topps is the only publicly owned major baseball card manufacturer. Because Topps is a public company, it is easy to see through its published sales figures that Topps has been very successful for the past few years. Topps continues to be committed to producing major baseball card sets each year and has remained in a leadership role, despite much recent competition. The future of Topps looks very bright.

Fleer

The Fleer Corporation was founded in 1914 by Frank H. Fleer, but the roots of the company go back to 1849. In 1849, Otto Holstein, the father-in-law of Fleer, organized a company to produce flavoring extracts. Fleer, who was born in 1860, took over the company in the 1880s and began making gum in 1885. The company invented the first bubble gum in the early 1900s and marketed it as Blibber-Blubber. Blibber-Blubber was not a major success, as it was too sticky and did not hold together well. It could be used to blow bubbles, but the bubbles had a tendency to burst easily and stick very stubbornly to the chewer's face. Frank's brother Henry invented Chiclets in the early 1900s for the company, and they turned out to be very popular. Fleer sold the company to the Sen Sen Company (later sold to the American Chicle Company) in 1909 and then went into a brief retirement.

In 1914, Fleer started a new chewing gum company, the Frank H. Fleer Corporation, and this is the company that now exists as simply the Fleer Corporation. The company made many attempts to develop new types of gum, but none was very successful. Frank Fleer died in 1921, and his work was carried on by his

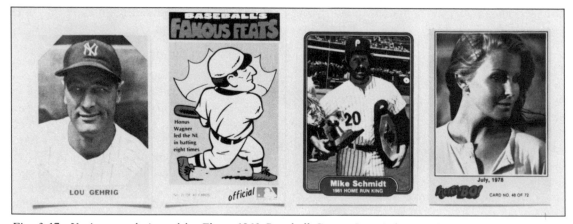

Fig. 3-17. Various cards issued by Fleer: 1960 Baseball Greats Lou Gehrig, 1973 Famous Feats Honus Wagner, 1982 Mike Schmidt, 1981 Here's Bo (Bo Derek).

son-in-law, Gilbert Mustin. In 1928, a 23-year-old employee named Walter Diemer invented the first successful bubble gum ever made by anyone. Diemer had no knowledge of chemistry and found the right combination of ingredients purely by trial and error. The bubble gum he created made huge bubbles and peeled gently and easily from the chewer's face upon bursting. When the first batch of the new bubble gum was made, the only food coloring at hand was pink, and this is the main reason why almost all bubble gum today is found in this color. The new bubble gum was called Dubble Bubble, and proved to be hugely successful.

The first set of trading cards ever produced by Fleer was a set of movie star cards, probably produced in the 1920s (*American Card Catalog* number E241). In the early 1930s, many of Fleer's competitors began issuing baseball cards with gum, yet Fleer did not follow suit. This may have been because Dubble Bubble was already hugely successful without the use of premiums. In any event, Fleer did not issue another card set until 1938, when it issued a set of "Cops and Robbers" cards. Fleer's first baseball card set did not come until 1959, when their Ted Williams set appeared.

With the Ted Williams set, Fleer became the first serious threat to the Topps dominance in the baseball card market since Topps had purchased Bowman. Fleer had signed Williams to an exclusive contract, and he did not appear as an active player on Topps cards after 1958. Fleer had a problem with card #68 in its 1959 set, reportedly because someone pictured with Williams was under contract to Topps. The card was withdrawn from the set shortly after release and is very scarce today.

Fleer issued several small sets of cards in the early 1960s featuring all-time great baseball players and an abbreviated set of current major league player cards. From 1969 through 1976 Fleer issued some other small sets featuring baseball stadiums, the World Series, famous baseball events, and pioneers of baseball.

In 1975 Fleer instituted a lawsuit against Topps that resulted in the end of the dominance of Topps in the baseball card market. Since 1981, Fleer and other companies have issued large sets of current baseball player cards in competition with Topps (Fig. 3-17).

In addition to baseball cards, Fleer has also produced many other types of card sets over the years. For example, Fleer issued sets

*Fig. 3-18. Various Leaf and Donruss card issues: 1948 Leaf Paul (Dizzy) Trout, 1983 Donruss Baseball (San Diego Chicken), 1986 Leaf Bert Blyleven, 1982 Donruss "M*A*S*H."*

of Three Stooges cards in 1959 and 1965, as well as sets for TV shows such as "Gomer Pyle," "Hogan's Heroes," and "McHale's Navy." Fleer issued football and basketball cards in the early 1960s, as well as another basketball set in the mid-1980s. Fleer appears to be committed to continuing to produce yearly baseball card sets and other types of card sets in the future.

Donruss/Leaf

When Fleer won its lawsuit with Topps in 1980, the decision stated that other companies could negotiate with the MLBPA to issue baseball card sets with gum. As a result of this decision, the Donruss Company of Memphis, Tennessee, applied for and was granted a license to produce baseball cards. The first Donruss baseball card set was issued in 1981 with bubble gum.

The Donruss Company was formed in 1958 and was named for its two owners, Don and Russ Wiener. Before 1958 it was known as the Thomas Wiener Candy Company. Though Donruss had never before issued a baseball card set, the company was not a newcomer to the card-collecting world, as it had been is-

suing various nonsports card sets since the early 1960s. The first set of cards Donruss issued was probably a set of "Idiot" cards in 1961. Other Donruss sets have been based on television shows ("The Green Hornet," "The Monkees," "The Flying Nun," "The Six Million Dollar Man," "Dallas," "The Dukes of Hazzard," "Magnum"), movies (*Saturday Night Fever, Tron, The Dark Crystal*), musical groups (Freddie and the Dreamers, The Osmonds, Kiss), and various other subjects (Disneyland, Marvel Super Heroes, Elvis). Donruss also issued sets of Golf cards in 1981 and 1982 (Fig. 3-18).

When Donruss began making baseball cards, it tried to add some innovation to its sets. In the first set in 1981, Donruss issued several different cards for some of the stars of the day. This was unusual because in most baseball card sets there is only one card per player, although sometimes special cards such as All-Star or special achievement cards are used to picture star players more than once. Donruss also issued cards of the Famous Chicken, which was unusual because team mascots are rarely seen on baseball cards. In its 1982 set, Donruss began issuing its "Diamond King" cards, featuring an artist's ren-

Fig. 3-19. Donruss includes original artwork by Baseball Hall of Fame artist Dick Perez on some cards. 1983 Hall of Fame Heroes Yogi Berra, 1988 Donruss Diamond King Mark McGwire, 1983 Donruss baseball card featuring artist Dick Perez.

dition of one star per team. Donruss has continued issuing Diamond Kings every year since. The Diamond Kings were a nice innovation, since almost all present-day baseball cards feature photographs instead of original artwork. For the 1985 set, Donruss included four bonus cards that could be cut off the bottom of the wax pack boxes. Topps, Fleer, and Score all followed suit in later years (Fig. 3-19).

After 1981, Donruss was unable to issue baseball cards with gum because of the reversal of the court decision which had allowed the company to issue its initial set. Since 1982, Donruss has been issuing cards with puzzle pieces.

In 1985, Donruss was purchased along with several other candy companies by a Finnish conglomerate. The companies were all merged together as Leaf, Inc. The Leaf name was taken from one of the other companies that was purchased, the Leaf Confectionary Company of Chicago, Illinois. Leaf Confectionary was another candy and gum company which twice issued baseball card sets. In 1948–1949, Leaf issued a set of current player cards that also featured a retired Babe Ruth. The set was skip-numbered in a way that was very confusing to card collectors. In 1960, Leaf issued a black-and-white set of current player cards. Most of the cards in that set featured marginal players.

Since the merger, the Donruss name has remained on the U.S. baseball card sets, and production of the cards has continued to take place in Memphis. From 1985 to 1988, the company issued Canadian versions of its baseball card sets, and those bear the Leaf name. Donruss continues to make baseball cards that are well received by collectors each year. It appears that Donruss will be making baseball card sets for a long time.

Score/SportFlics

The SportFlics cards first appeared on the baseball card scene in 1986 with an issue of 200 cards. In 1988, the first set of 660 Score cards was released. Both of these card sets were created and distributed by the same group of companies. Optigraphics of Grand Prairie, Texas, is responsible for the design and production of the cards, while Amurol distributes the cards to retail stores around the country and Major League Marketing distributes them to baseball card dealers.

SportFlics are ''Magic Motion'' cards, that is, each card can be tilted at different angles

Fig. 3-20. Score and SportFlics cards: 1988 Score Fred Lynn, 1989 Score Jose Canseco, 1988 Score card back of Graig Nettles, 1989 SportFlics card back of Roger Clemens.

to display three different pictures. Some cards feature different views of a batter's swing or a pitcher's delivery to make the action come alive. SportFlics baseball cards have a thick plastic coating, making them reminiscent of Kellogg's baseball cards of the 1970s and early 1980s.

Since 1976, new sets of SportFlics cards have continued to be released annually. The cards are issued in tamperproof Mylar packages with a suggested retail price of 59 cents for three cards. At approximately 20 cents a card, SportFlics cards are much more expensive than Topps, Donruss, Fleer, or Score cards, which usually sell for about 3 cents per card (Fig. 3-20).

The first set of Score cards issued in 1988 was an attempt to compete directly with Topps and the other major card manufacturers. The Score cards were a standard card set priced about the same as the competitors' cards. The 1988 Score cards feature high-quality action photographs on the fronts along with full-color backs containing stats, a highly informative player biography, and a small portrait photograph. The 1988 Score cards were issued in tamperproof packs, but the cards within could be viewed before the package was opened. The

1989 packs remained tamperproof, but the cards within were hidden.

Several smaller sets produced by Optigraphics have been sold by Major League Marketing only through baseball card dealers, and mail-in sets of Young Superstars are advertised on Score wrappers.

Optigraphics has put great emphasis on creating quality baseball cards. Though only recently established, the company has become a force in the baseball card business. The 1988 Score set was very well received by collectors, although it may have had an adverse effect on their 1988 SportFlics set, which was largely ignored. Because of their unusual design and high price, SportFlics cards are not very popular with baseball card collectors. Some collectors speculate that Score cards will eventually cause SportFlics cards to be phased out, though the company insists that both products will continue in the future.

Upper Deck

The first set of 800 Upper Deck baseball cards was released in 1989. The Upper Deck Company, of Anaheim, California, was created with the sole purpose of creating and sell-

65

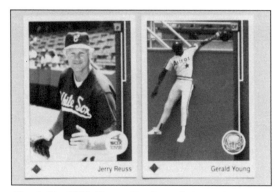

Fig. 3-21. 1989 Upper Deck cards (premier issue): Jerry Reuss, Gerald Young.

ing baseball cards. Upper Deck cards are sold in tamperproof packages and contain 3-D team logo holograms as well as baseball cards. Each card has a small hologram on the back.

Upper Deck addressed some of the common complaints about baseball cards with its first set. Upper Deck issued its cards in tamperproof packages, with none of the cards showing through, to prevent unscrupulous people from opening the packages and substituting bad cards for good. Upper Deck included a hologram on the back of each card as a deterrent to counterfeiters. Also, Upper Deck card numbers are in large print. (Small card numbers are a common complaint of baseball card dealers who sort through large numbers of cards to put together complete sets.) (Fig. 3-21)

The main drawback to Upper Deck cards is the price. They cost approximately twice as much as similar cards issued by Topps, Fleer, Donruss, and Score. However, the cards seem to be getting favorable collector reaction despite the cost, because they are perceived as a quality product.

MSA

Michael Schechter Associates (MSA) has been creating baseball cards for many years as promotional items for other products. The company has produced cards that have been issued with such products as potato chips, breakfast cereal, iced tea, popcorn, ice cream, candy bars, beef jerky, and bread. MSA has even produced a set to be given away with haircuts. MSA has never issued a set on its own, so it's hard to predict where the cards will show up next.

MSA has been licensed by the MLBPA to produce baseball cards for many years, but has never obtained a license from Major League Baseball. Because of this, most MSA baseball cards feature players with airbrushed caps to hide the team logos. Most of the sets contain between 20 to 30 cards. Many MSA cards are issued in a round form, also referred to as baseball discs.

MSA created its first set of baseball cards in 1976. It produced a set of 70 discs that were sold with several different products from various regions of the country. The same pictures were on the fronts, with different advertising on the backs. Crane Potato Chips discs and Isaly discs were among the more popular. Baseball card dealers obtained large numbers of these discs, decreasing their value.

When MSA creates a card set for another company, complete control of the distribution of the cards is in the hands of the company that has purchased them. Many of the companies that have issued MSA cards have put tight controls on their issues to prevent card dealers from getting large quantities. They know that their promotions will be more successful if collectors are forced to buy the product to get the cards, rather than going to their local card dealer. As a result, some of the MSA issues are among the more difficult recent baseball cards to obtain (Fig. 3-22).

The market that MSA caters to is currently shared only by Topps among the major card producers. Through 1988, no other major baseball card company had produced card sets

Fig. 3-22. MSA baseball cards: 1976 Crane Potato Chips Johnny Bench, 1988 Fantastic Sam's Kirby Puckett, 1988 King B Wally Joyner.

for other companies. MSA has been very aggressive in this market in recent years. For example, in 1987 MSA produced different sets to be sold via Kraft macaroni and cheese, Bohemian Hearth bread, Cains potato chips, Jiffy Pop popcorn, M&M's candy, Ralston Purina Company breakfast cereal, Burger King restaurants, and several brands of iced tea. In 1988, one of MSA's sets was issued with Nestlés candy bars, a company that had twice issued Topps-produced card sets.

MSA baseball cards are a throwback to the days when all baseball cards were issued as promotional items for some type of product. Many collectors find them challenging to collect because of the difficulty in getting them.

Other Companies Producing Baseball Cards

Topps, Fleer, Donruss, Score/SportFlics, Upper Deck, and MSA are the major baseball card manufacturers these days, but there are also others. Some companies design and issue their own promotional baseball cards instead of hiring Topps or MSA to do it for them. Some

very attractive cards are done this way. Companies that have produced their own cards in recent years include Mother's Cookies, Granny Goose potato chips, Big League Chew gum, and many team-issued cards. The Mother's Cookies cards of the 1980s are particularly beautiful. They feature rounded corners, a high-gloss finish, and crisp, bright, borderless photographs. Mother's has produced separate card sets for various teams and usually distributes them on a promotional day at the ballpark.

There are also several companies producing minor league cards that are available at minor league ballparks or through baseball card dealers. Collectors Marketing Corp. (CMC, formerly TCMA, which stood for The Card Memorabilia Associates) has been producing these sets for the longest time, with sets stretching from 1972 to the present. Other companies that have been issuing minor league cards in recent years include The Star Company, ProCards, Pacific Trading Cards, and various others (Fig. 3-23).

In addition to minor league cards, Pacific Trading Cards of Edmunds, Washington, has also issued some other types of baseball card sets, including Baseball Legends trading cards and a card set for the movie *Eight Men Out*.

Fig. 3-23. Card issues from various companies: 1986 Big League Chew Gum Mickey Mantle, 1988 Mother's Cookies Will Clark, 1988 CMC Denver Zephyrs Billy Jo Robidoux.

The Baseball Legends cards feature retired baseball greats and are issued in wax packs.

With the increasing popularity of baseball cards in the past decade, it seems as if new manufacturers are producing and attempting to produce new baseball card sets each year. Watch for other new companies entering the field in future years.

The Score Board and Others Who Resell Old Cards

In the past few years, a new kind of baseball card product has begun to appear in retail stores around the country: old baseball cards repackaged and sold by a company other than the original manufacturer. These packages usually contain an assortment of cards from different years and different manufacturers that are a year old or more. The cards that are included seldom contain superstar or top rookie players because the companies that repackage them have removed all of those cards to sell to other markets. These repackaged assort-

ments are usually sold for a price that far exceeds the retail price in the year of manufacture. There are several companies selling cards in this way. One of the leaders is a company called The Score Board, Inc.

The Score Board was organized to buy and sell baseball cards and other sports memorabilia and to develop and market its own line of sports-related products. The thing that sets The Score Board apart from other baseball card dealers is that the company went public in August of 1987, with an initial offering of 77 million shares of common stock. Because of its status as a public company, The Score Board has much more capital than other baseball card dealers.

One of the master plans of The Score Board is as follows:

1. Acquire mass quantities of baseball cards directly from the manufacturers.
2. Sort through the cards, separating the superstars and top rookies from the rest.
3. Sell the superstars and top rookies to base-

ball card dealers and investors for a substantial immediate profit.

4. Repackage the rest of the cards and sell them in later years as old collectible cards with highly marked-up prices.

In the present baseball card market, this strategy appears to be extremely intelligent and lucrative. Other dealers have followed this same strategy for the past few years, but nobody has attempted to follow it on the same scale as The Score Board. The Score Board currently has a contract with Topps to acquire 2,000 cases of Topps baseball cards each quarter of the year. This computes to 24 million cards per quarter—almost 100 million cards per year.

The Score Board has been successful in following through on its business plan in the brief time it has been in business. It will be interesting to see what new products the company develops and to see if its strategies will continue to be profitable in the future.

The Organized Hobby

Baseball card collectors of today have a vast amount of information about the hobby at their disposal. There are huge card collections on display at several prominent museums, thousands of baseball card shows every year, an impressive selection of reference books available, and some quality magazines devoted entirely to baseball cards and other sports collectibles.

Major Card Collections

Baseball card collectors everywhere are fortunate that two of the finest card collections ever assembled are available for public viewing. The Jefferson Burdick collection is housed in a New York museum; the Larry Fritsch collection is scheduled to go on display in the summer of 1990 at a Wisconsin museum, after spending 1988 at a museum in Cooperstown. In addition, the National Baseball Hall of Fame also contains its own collection of baseball cards.

The Jefferson Burdick Collection

The Jefferson Burdick collection of paper Americana is housed in one of the most impressive museums in the country, the Metropolitan Museum of Art in New York City. The collection contains items dating from the mid-1800s through the early 1960s. It represents the life work of a man devoted almost completely to collecting and cataloguing trading cards and other types of paper collectibles.

Jefferson Burdick was the pioneer of organized baseball card collecting. Born in 1900, Burdick became interested in collecting cards in the 1910 era, when there was a boom of baseball card issues. In a 1955 article in the Syracuse *Herald Journal,* Burdick recalled collecting cigarette cards as a child. "Practically every small boy saved these kind of cards. We made our dads use certain brands whether they liked them or not." By the mid-1930s, he had amassed a large collection of cards, mostly by advertising in general hobby magazines and

Fig. 4-1. Some of the pioneers of card collecting. From left to right, Woody Gelman, Jefferson Burdick, Charles Bray, and Gene DeNardo. Photo courtesy of The Old Judge.

in other places. Burdick began sharing his knowledge with other card collectors when he published some early tobacco card checklists in a general hobby magazine in 1936. This stimulated a lot of interest, and in 1937 he began publishing his own newsletter called *The Card Collector's Bulletin* (Fig. 4-1).

It should be noted that Burdick had no special interest in baseball. His real interest was in trading cards of all types, and baseball subjects just happened to be pictured on many of the cards he collected. His collection consisted of every type of card he could discover, and he put no special emphasis on acquiring baseball players over other card subjects. He didn't even limit himself to trading cards, as he amassed large quantities of other types of paper collectibles, such as postcards, greeting cards, valentines, and stereoscope cards.

In 1939, Burdick published the first catalog book for trading cards called *The United States Card Collector's Catalog*. In 1946, Burdick updated his catalog and renamed it *The American Card Catalog*. He subsequently updated the book every few years, and his final updated version was published in 1960. This landmark book was reprinted in 1967 and was out of print until 1988, when it was reprinted

by the Card Collectors' Company. *The American Card Catalog* contained listings for all of the known card sets, with baseball card sets as well as other sport and non-sport sets listed. As discussed earlier, this book established the first numbering system for categorizing card sets. For example, "T206" was *The American Card Catalog* number for the 1909–11 white-bordered set of baseball tobacco cards. Burdick made an attempt to establish values for the cards by listing the value for an average card in each set. There were no checklists of the cards within the sets, and very few special listings for the more valuable cards. Though pricing information was presented, the main purpose of *The American Card Catalog* was simply to inform collectors about what was available.

When collectors look at the pricing information in the 1960 version of *The American Card Catalog* today, the prices seem ridiculously low. Cards from almost every baseball card set were listed at less than $1 each. For example, 1910 T206 cards were listed at 10 cents each, 1887 N172 Old Judge cards were valued at 25 cents each, and 1952 Topps high numbers were listed at 30 cents apiece. The highest priced card in the whole catalog was the T206 Honus Wagner, valued at $50. Though the prices were low, they reflected the low demand of the times. There were very few serious baseball card collectors in 1960, and the low prices represented the legitimate market value for the cards. Burdick himself worked very hard to keep card prices low, as he was afraid that card collecting would become as overly commercialized as the coin and stamp collecting hobbies. He hoped card collecting would remain an enjoyable, affordable hobby for everyone who wished to participate in it.

In 1947, Burdick approached the Metropolitan Museum of Art in New York City about permanently displaying his enormous card collection for the benefit of the public. Though

Fig. 4-2. The Metropolitan Museum of Art.

not particularly interested at first, the museum later agreed to house the cards (Fig. 4-2).

Burdick had put together possibly the greatest collection of trading cards in the world, with over 300,000 items. There are complete sets of most of the baseball cards issued from the 1880s up until 1960. There are many extremely rare cards, including a large collection of the Old Judge cards from the late 1880s. For display purposes, Burdick decided to mount his entire collection in large albums. He mounted the cards himself, in the same order as his *American Card Catalog* listings. There were no plastic pages available at the time, so he glued or hinged the cards to the albums. Mounting the cards was a very slow and painful process for Burdick, since he suffered from severe arthritis. He slowly delivered albums of cards to the museum from 1948 through 1959.

In 1959, realizing that his health was deteriorating, Burdick began to work full-time on the project. He moved to New York and was given a small corner in the Print Department of the museum in which to work. Burdick had completed 34 albums when he began to work full-time on the project, and he completed another 360 albums over the next few years, with the last card being mounted in January of 1963.

Burdick himself was not sure whether he would live to finish the project. With the same drive that enabled him to amass such a fabulous collection of cards, he pushed himself to live long enough to complete what he had undertaken to do. When the last card was mounted, Burdick considered his life work to be complete. Two months later, he died.

The fabulous Jefferson Burdick collection is still housed at the Metropolitan Museum of Art. Viewing is available to the public by appointment only, and only by individuals or small groups. Burdick himself established the rules for viewing the collection, which include no pens being allowed in the room and other similar restrictions designed to help safeguard the collection.

The Larry Fritsch Collection

In the summer of 1988, Larry Fritsch opened a museum near the Baseball Hall of Fame in Cooperstown, New York, to display his impressive baseball card collection. The Larry Fritsch Baseball Card Collection was the first museum in the country devoted solely to baseball cards.

Larry Fritsch has been well known in the card-collecting hobby for years because of his large mail-order baseball card business. Like many collectors, Fritsch started his baseball card business as a means of making a profit from his hobby. In 1970, the business had grown so well that he decided to quit his job and devote all his efforts to it. At the time, nobody else was supporting themselves solely from baseball cards, making him the first full-time baseball card dealer. The business now contains a stock of over 34 million cards, with unopened cases of Topps cards dating back to the late 1960s.

In addition to selling cards produced by others, Fritsch has issued some baseball card sets on his own. He issued 22 minor league

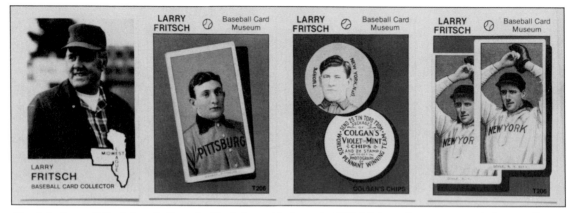

Fig. 4-3. Larry Fritsch baseball cards. The left card is from the 1982 Midwest League set and shows collector Larry Fritsch. The other three cards are 1988 promotional cards for the Larry Fritsch museum, including cards featuring the 1910 T206 Honus Wagner card, the 1913 Colgan's Chips Jim Thorpe card, and the 1910 T206 Joe Doyle variations. The only known copies of the Thorpe card and the Doyle NAT'L variation are on display at the Larry Fritsch museum.

sets for the Midwest League in 1982 and 1983. He also has put out card sets called "One Year Winners." The One Year Winners cards feature players that never appeared on a baseball card because they had only very brief major league careers. For example, Eddie Gaedel, the midget who appeared in one game in 1951, has a card in this set. Fritsch has also issued a set of eight cards commemorating the grand opening of his museum that show pictures of some of the rare cards from his collection (Fig. 4-3).

Fritsch has been continuously collecting baseball cards since 1948, when he was still a child. Even after he began selling baseball cards for a living, he never parted with any cards from his personal collection. His collection now contains over 1 million cards, including complete sets of almost everything. He owns most of the rare cards in the hobby, including the only known copies of several cards.

Fritsch decided to open his museum because he wanted to share his collection with others. Because of the rapid rise in baseball

card prices in recent years, many of his rare cards were stored in bank safe deposit boxes where nobody could enjoy them. The location of the museum was chosen because of its close proximity to the Baseball Hall of Fame. Over 281,000 people visited the Hall of Fame in 1987 to view baseball history, and it seemed only natural that a large portion of those people would also be interested in baseball card history.

The Larry Fritsch museum opened in Cooperstown in the summer of 1988. It was an immediate success, drawing 34,000 visitors in three months. Despite that success, Fritsch was unhappy about living in New York, away from his family in Wisconsin. In the fall of 1988, Fritsch permanently closed his Cooperstown museum and moved back to Wisconsin, with plans to open a new museum in that state in the summer of 1990.

Because the collection is so enormous, it was displayed at Cooperstown on a rotating basis, with about 20,000 cards on display at one time. There would have to have been about

50 times more space to exhibit the entire collection at once. There were future plans to create a baseball card viewing room where visitors could view any specific cards of their choice, with the cards cross-referenced by team, player, and number.

The Fritsch collection spans the entire history of baseball cards, from the 1880s to the present. Fritsch made the recently discovered Doyle T206 variation card the symbol of his museum. The first two known copies of the Doyle variation with "NAT'L" in the caption are owned and were displayed by Fritsch. (At least two more copies have been reported by other collectors since Fritsch's cards were discovered.) Other rare cards on display included the famed T206 Honus Wagner and the Plank and Magie cards.

In addition to the museum, there was also a gift store and baseball card shop. The gift store featured T-shirts, posters, glassware, books, videos, and other similar items, while the card shop featured a wide assortment of cards and accessories for collectors of all levels. Larry Fritsch plans to reopen his museum in Stevens Point, Wisconsin, in the summer of 1990. See Appendix E for more information.

The National Baseball Hall of Fame

The National Baseball Hall of Fame in Cooperstown, New York, is a place every baseball fan would love to visit. Dedicated in 1939, its purpose is to house historic artifacts from the game of baseball. Each year there is an election to induct former players and other baseball personnel into the Hall of Fame, and each member has his own exhibit.

The Hall of Fame relies entirely on donations for acquiring new items. When a baseball milestone occurs, a representative of the Hall usually contacts the team to request a relevant item. Though occasionally a player will choose not to give up the item, such a case is rare. The Hall of Fame usually gets what it wants. In addition to requested items, hundreds of other artifacts are donated annually.

Cooperstown was chosen as the site for the Hall of Fame because of its historical significance. Though the evidence is far from conclusive, legend has it that the first game of baseball was organized by Abner Doubleday and played in farmer Elihu Phinney's cow pasture in Cooperstown in 1839. When plans for baseball's 100th anniversary were under way, Cooperstown was chosen as the site for the Hall of Fame. The Hall is located one block from Doubleday Field, which is the old site of Phinney's pasture.

The Hall of Fame owns and exhibits some baseball cards, though its collection is far from complete. It does own and display a copy of the famous Honus Wagner T206 card, donated by well-known collector Barry Halper. The Hall of Fame's reliance on donations has prevented it from compiling a better baseball card collection. Also, baseball cards are of secondary importance to the Hall of Fame; its first interest is in the uniforms and equipment of the stars of baseball.

Each year the Hall's busiest time is the weekend of the Hall of Fame inductions and the Hall of Fame Game. People travel from all parts of the country for the festivities, including most of the living Hall of Famers who make the journey to welcome new members. The baseball game played at Doubleday Field is an exhibition game between two major league teams.

In addition to the museum, the Hall of Fame has a gift shop and a mail-order catalog. Among the many souvenirs of interest to collectors are Hall of Fame postcards and Perez-Steele Galleries art cards. The Hall of Fame is open year-round, though summer is the peak season.

Baseball Card Shows

In the late 1960s and early 1970s, the first baseball card shows began to appear around the country. The early shows were usually small gatherings of collectors held at a local high school or meeting hall. Most of the card dealers at these shows were collectors who were trying to sell off some of their duplicates so that they could buy more cards.

At the time of the early shows, there were probably no more than a handful of full-time baseball card dealers in the entire country. Most of the sellers simply brought some cards in old shoe boxes. There was a general pricing structure for most cards; however, there were no price guides. These early shows were a great success because collectors were starved for the opportunity to acquire such a wide variety of cards.

As the years wore on, baseball card shows became bigger and more professional. Some people began making a lot of money, and many new people became card dealers and show promoters. The 1979 publication of *The Sport Americana Baseball Card Price Guide* gave dealers a standard price structure for most of the popular baseball cards. As the 1980s rolled around, most of the shoe boxes were disappearing from card shows and were being replaced with glass cases.

The addition of Fleer and Donruss on the baseball card scene in 1981 coincided with a large increase in baseball card dealers. Sud-denly there were three times as many cards around, and many people rushed to sell them. More and more shows were being held and the baseball card hobby was becoming a big business. Today, there are thousands of baseball card shows held each year. As an example of their abundance, there were 451 different shows scheduled to be held around the country in June 1988, according to the convention calendar in *Sports Collectors Digest*.

The National Convention

The first National Sports Collectors Convention was held in 1980 in Los Angeles. The original concept was to create a baseball card show that was national in scope, that would attract most of the major dealers in the country, and that would move to different geographical regions and be run by different promoters each year. The first National Convention was a great success, and there have been bigger and better National Conventions just about every year since. The cities that have hosted the National Conventions are as follows:

1980   Los Angeles, California
1981   Plymouth, Michigan
1982   St. Louis, Missouri
1983   Chicago, Illinois
1984   Parsippany, New Jersey

1985   Los Angeles, California
1986   Dallas, Texas
1987   San Francisco, California
1988   Atlantic City, New Jersey
1989   Chicago, Illinois
1990   Arlington, Texas

In the early years of the National Convention, anyone wishing to host the following year's show could make a presentation at the current convention, and a vote by the collectors and dealers present would decide the winner. As the convention grew bigger and more important, a rules committee was established to try to protect the event from falling into the hands of a dishonest or incompetent promoter. In 1984, a National Convention committee was elected from within the hobby and National Convention bylaws were written. It is hoped that this will protect the integrity of the National Convention and keep it flourishing for many years.

Some of the things that make the National Convention stand out above other card shows include a huge location, a top-caliber nationwide dealer list, a three- or four-day show length, huge attendance, seminars conducted by hobby experts, a banquet with big name guests, and a convention program. In recent years, the National Convention has begun attracting the interest of corporate sponsors.

Collectors attending past nationals have often been in awe of the vast quantity and exceptional quality of the baseball cards that can be found. The National Convention seems to be getting better every year. If you get the chance to go to one, it will be an experience you won't soon forget.

Baseball Card Books

There have been some fine baseball card reference books written, most of which have been released in recent years. As discussed earlier, the first baseball card book was *The American Card Catalog,* by Jefferson Burdick.

Some of the other important baseball card books include *The Sports Collectors Bible, The Sport Americana Baseball Card Price Guide, The Encyclopedia of Baseball Cards* series of books, the Krause Publications *Sports Collectors Digest Baseball Card Price Guide* and *Standard Catalog of Baseball Cards, Topps Baseball Cards* and *Classic Baseball Cards* from Warner Books, *The Baseball Card Dealer Directory,* and *The American Premium Guide to Baseball Cards.* Address information for ordering these books can be found in Appendix D of this book.

The Sports Collectors Bible

The Sports Collectors Bible, written by Bert Randolph Sugar and published by the Wallace-Homestead Book Company, was the first major card-collecting book to appear since Jefferson Burdick's *American Card Catalog.* First published in 1975, *The Sports Collectors Bible* provided checklists and price information for all of the most commonly collected sports items. Included in the book were listings and approximate values for baseball cards, pins, postcards, autographs, books, guides, yearbooks, matchbook covers, APBA game cards, programs and scorecards, ticket stubs, and uniforms. In addition, the names and addresses of the major hobby publications of the time were listed along with a registry of over

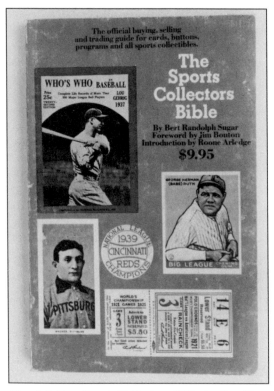

Fig. 4-4. The Sports Collectors Bible *by Bert Randolph Sugar (1975 edition).*

1,000 collector names, addresses, and areas of interest (Fig. 4-4).

Each section of *The Sports Collectors Bible* was written by one of the leading experts in the field, including a section on trading cards, by Larry Fritsch; a section on early candy and gum cards, by Richard Egan; and a section on matchbook covers, by Frank Nagy. Included was a short write-up on each particular subject followed by listings of the collectibles and price ranges.

The baseball card section takes up well over half of the book. Most of the baseball card sets covered in the book are provided with a checklist of every card in the set, along with approximate values for cards from the set. There is little indication given that con-

dition has a significant effect on card values. There are no values listed for individual cards except in the case of very rare or valuable cards. In those cases, there are special notes listed below the common values. If the set contains variations, these are also covered below the values section.

There are no checklists for Topps cards, but only a summary of each set. Listing all of the 15,000+ Topps cards issued up until 1975 would have taken up too much space.

It is interesting to look at some of the values of baseball cards in 1975. For example, in the T206 set, individual cards were valued at 50 cents to $1 each, and the Honus Wagner card was listed at $1,500. By contrast, the 1989 *Baseball Card Price Guide* published by *Sports Collectors Digest* lists common T206 cards in near-mint condition at $50 and the Honus Wagner card at $95,000. Most other cards are also valued substantially higher today. Even though the prices listed for baseball cards in *The Sports Collectors Bible* are not very relevant today, they are useful for charting trends in the values of baseball cards over the years.

The selection of baseball card sets listed in *The Sports Collectors Bible* is very interesting. There are many sets listed that are not commonly found in the price guides that are issued today. For example, some of the unusual sets listed include Meadow Gold Dairy cards of 1964, Burger Beer Cleveland Indians cards of 1959–1965, Tacoma Bank of Washington minor league cards of 1960 and 1961, Shopsy's Frankfurters minor league cards of 1960, Fleer 1969 Stadium cards, and Fleer 1970 and 1971 World Series cards.

The collectors registry in the back of the book was a free listing of every sports collector that sent in a request for inclusion. Collectors were encouraged to write in and be included through many advertisements in the hobby magazines before the book was published. Over 1,000 collectors are listed along with their ad-

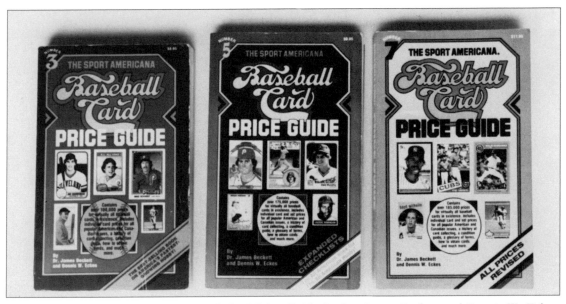

Fig. 4-5. The Sport Americana Baseball Card Price Guide *by Dr. James Beckett and Dennis W. Eckes. Pictured are issue number 3 (1981), number 5 (1983), and number 7 (1985).*

dresses and collecting interests. In the years since the initial printing of *The Sports Collectors Bible,* there have been at least three other printings of the book. While this book is still of interest, the price guides of today have greatly reduced its value as a reference book.

The Sport Americana Baseball Card Price Guide

The Sport Americana Baseball Card Price Guide, initially written by Dr. James Beckett and Dennis Eckes, was first published in 1979. A revised *Baseball Card Price Guide* has been issued every year since. In recent years, Beckett has become the sole author (Fig. 4-5). This landmark book was the first baseball card *price guide* ever published. It lists every card in each set along with their values in three different conditions. Almost all of the most popular baseball card sets are listed in these books, though some of the more uncommon sets are

listed in some editions but not in others. All of the Topps, Bowman, Fleer, Donruss, Sportflics, and Score cards are listed in each edition.

While *The American Card Catalog* brought the card collecting hobby out of the dark ages and *The Sports Collectors Bible* continued to provide baseball card collectors with important information, it remained for *The Sport Americana Baseball Card Price Guide* to really make baseball card collecting a major American hobby, ranking it with coins and stamps in collecting popularity. The reason this book was so important is that it gave price information for every individual card in each set listed, not just an approximate value for an average card in the set. Anyone who owned a baseball card could find out *exact* information about the value of the card, rather than just general information about it.

In addition to the lists of cards, there is a picture of the front and back of a sample card

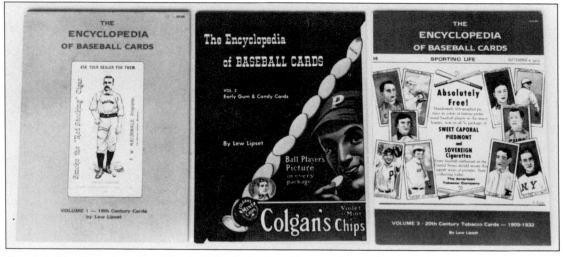

Fig. 4-6. The Encyclopedia of Baseball Cards *by Lew Lipset, volumes 1, 2, and 3.*

from each set listed. There are also a few pages of color pictures of various baseball cards. In the earlier issues there are some very interesting and informative articles, but these have been eliminated in recent years due to a lack of space.

The Baseball Card Price Guide is just one of many price guides put out by Sport Americana. Other titles include *The Baseball Memorabilia and Autograph Price Guide, The Price Guide to Baseball Collectibles, The Price Guide to the Non-Sport Cards, The Baseball Card Alphabetical Checklist, The Baseball Card Team Checklist, The Baseball Address List,* and *The Football, Hockey, Basketball and Boxing Card Price Guide.* In addition to the price guides, Sport Americana also published a pamphlet called *T206 The Monster.* Written by Bill Heitman, this pamphlet is devoted entirely to the T206 baseball card set of 1909–1911. The pamphlet discusses theories about the way the set was marketed and presents a thorough checklist that includes listings of the different backs that can be found with each card. All of these books are currently in print and can be found at many bookstores or can be ordered through mail-order dealers.

The Encyclopedia of Baseball Cards

Lew Lipset has written the first three of a proposed six installments of *The Encyclopedia of Baseball Cards.* The books provide detailed coverage of distinct classifications of early baseball cards. Volume 1 was published in 1983 and covers all nineteenth-century baseball cards. Volume 2, published in 1984, covers early candy and gum cards. Volume 3, published in 1986, covers twentieth-century tobacco cards from 1909 to 1932. Lipset has plans to write three more volumes, including Volume 4 on bakery and periodical issues, Volume 5 on gum cards from 1941 and earlier, and Volume 6 on miscellaneous cards issued up to 1941 that were not covered in his other volumes (Fig. 4-6).

Lipset is one of the foremost experts on early baseball card sets and has spent a great deal of time researching the material in his books. Lipset's books are really the first attempt to present an in-depth look at the earliest baseball card issues. In his books, Lipset presents checklists of all the known cards from every set covered, including all variations. He discusses how and when the set was distributed, along with which cards are scarce. Many of the older baseball card sets that are covered use the same pictures from other sets, and Lipset does a good job of discussing the relationships between the sets. He also presents pricing information. There are illustrations of the front and back of cards from every set, along with other interesting pictures, such as advertising that was used at the time for some of the early card sets.

There is very little concrete knowledge of many of the early sets that are covered in these books, so Lipset presents his own theories on some subjects. For example, he speculates as to why certain cards are tougher to find than others. By studying the players involved, he sometimes theorizes that cards for players that have been traded during the season might have been pulled from distribution. In the E90-1 set, he speculates that the set was distributed over several years, with some of the scarce cards being included only in the later years of the promotion. Lipset's theories are well researched and a very important aspect of his books.

Happily, all three of *The Encyclopedia of Baseball Cards* books are still in print and are available directly from the author. Lipset also publishes *The Old Judge,* a newsletter devoted to early baseball cards.

Krause Publication Books

In recent years, Krause Publications has been publishing baseball card reference books, in addition to their many baseball card magazines.

The Sports Collectors Digest Baseball Card Price Guide

The *Sports Collectors Digest Baseball Card Price Guide* was first released in 1987 by the writers at *Sports Collectors Digest* and is now updated annually. It contains basically the same information that is found in *The Sport Americana Baseball Card Price Guides.* There has been a major effort to include all of the variations from each set listed. As a result, the listings for many sets in the *Sports Collectors Digest Baseball Card Price Guide* are more complete than in *The Sport Americana Baseball Card Price Guide,* especially for the Kellogg's sets of the 1970s and early 1980s (Fig. 4-7).

The Standard Catalog of Baseball Cards

The Standard Catalog of Baseball Cards, edited by Dan Albaugh and published by Krause Publications in late 1988, is billed as "the most comprehensive price guide ever published." It contains price listings for more than 1,800 baseball card sets, many of which have never appeared in any other price guide. It is a major effort, with checklists and pricing information for almost every baseball card made from 1887 to the present.

One of the many highlights of this book is the section on Zeenut cards. Checklists, sample pictures, and prices for all of the Zeenut cards from 1911 to 1938 are included. This is the first major book to include these listings. Other books have overlooked these cards because of space considerations and because the cards picture minor leaguers (Fig. 4-8).

There is a large section at the back of the book covering minor league sets that have been produced from 1972 through 1988. Included are sets produced by TCMA, Cramer Sports Promotions, ProCards, Fritsch Cards, and others. It is an extensive listing, and this is the

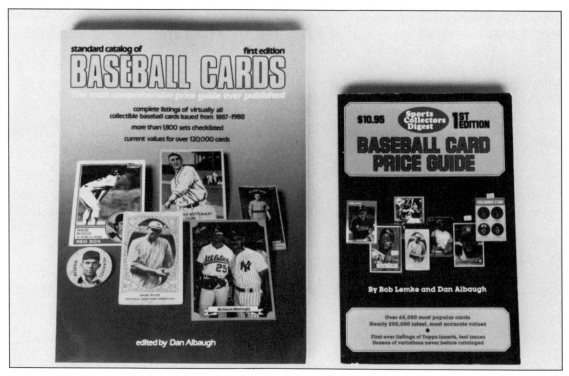

Fig. 4-7. The Standard Catalog of Baseball Cards *by Dan Albaugh and* The Sports Collectors Digest Baseball Card Price Guide *by Bob Lemke and Dan Albaugh. Both books are Krause publications.*

Fig. 4-8. Zeenut cards through the years: 1911 Mitze, 1916 Munsell, 1923 McAuliffe, 1937–38 Sprinz. Zeenut cards were issued every year from 1911 through 1938.

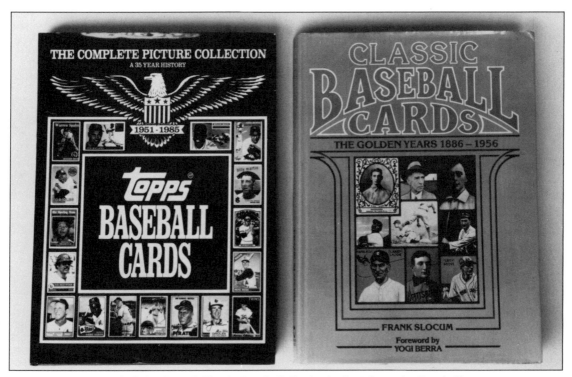

Fig. 4-9. Topps Baseball Cards *and* Classic Baseball Cards, *both with text by Frank Slocum.*

first time most of these sets have been listed in a major price guide.

Some of the other unusual or obscure sets that are listed include felt pennant sets of the mid-1930s; Jay Publishing Picture Pack photos of 1958 to 1965; Dixie lids from 1937 through 1953; baseball coins from Salada tea, Topps, and Armour hot dogs; and Wheaties cards from the 1930s.

Baseball card collectors that are only going to buy one reference book would do well to get this book. As the book advertises, listings for almost every baseball card set are present. Since this is only the first edition of this book, it is likely that the few sets that the book missed will appear in future editions.

Topps Baseball Cards and Classic Baseball Cards

Topps Baseball Cards, published by Warner Books in 1985 with text by Frank Slocum, contains full-color pictures of the fronts of Topps baseball cards issued from 1951 through 1985. Cards issued after 1985 have been pictured in separate update volumes. This is a fabulous book and is well worth the original retail price of $79.95. The cards pictured are from the major issues by Topps and the annual Topps Traded sets. There is a card pictured for every number issued from 1951 through 1985, along with some variations (although other variations are missing). All Topps inserts and minor sets are completely left out.

The cards in the book are separated by their year of issue, and there is accompanying text about each particular year. The highlights of each baseball season are covered, and notes are given about the Topps set from each year. There is also a short trivia quiz for each year, with the answer being one of the players in that year's set (Fig. 4-9). This book contains an interesting look at Topps baseball cards through the years. If you need to see what a particular Topps card looks like, this is a fantastic reference.

Classic Baseball Cards, published in 1988 by Warner Books, is presented in a style similar to that of *Topps Baseball Cards* and contains full-color pictures of most of the important card sets printed from the 1880s through 1956. This is another spectacular book, with full-color pictures of over 10,000 of the earliest baseball cards. Most of the early sets are pictured, including 1880s tobacco cards, cards from the 1909–1915 era, Goudeys, Bowmans, and many others. This book retails for $79.95.

The Baseball Card Dealer Directory

The 1988 Baseball Card and Collectibles Dealer Directory, written by Jim Wright and Jean-Paul Emard and published by Meckler Books, was the first directory of baseball card dealers ever published in book form. The first edition contained listings for more than 1,100 baseball card dealers. A new 1989 edition was renamed *The Baseball Card Dealer Directory.* In the book, baseball card dealers are listed under four separate indexes. The main index is an alphabetical directory of all of the dealers by business name. This listing includes the address, phone number, and specialties of the dealers. Card dealers are also indexed by spe-

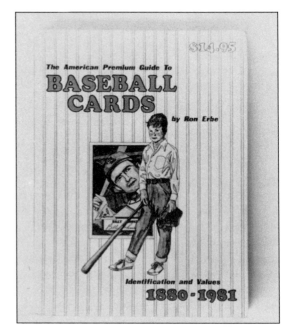

Fig. 4-10. The American Premium Guide to Baseball Cards *by Ron Erbe.*

cialty, geographical location, and dealer's last name.

The first edition of this book does not contain a complete listing of all baseball card dealers, but it is a good start. As the book becomes better known, future editions will probably contain more complete listings.

The American Premium Guide to Baseball Cards

The American Premium Guide to Baseball Cards was written by Ron Erbe and published in 1982. This was a very fine book that probably got lost in the shuffle. The book contains checklists and pricing information for almost every set of baseball cards from the 1880s through 1981. In addition, there is an alphabetical listing of baseball players cross-referenced with a list of the cards on which they appear. This listing includes all players, from those appearing on nineteenth-century tobacco cards up to players appearing on Topps cards.

This book contains one of the most thorough sections on nineteenth-century cards that has ever been written. The nineteenth-century section of the book was written by Keith Mitchell, who owns one of the largest known collections of the Old Judge cards. There is a complete discussion about how the cards were issued, and the checklists include listings for each of the many poses that are available for

most players (Fig. 4-10). There are also complete checklists of many early issues that are not covered in most of the baseball card price guides, including most of the minor league tobacco and candy cards from the 1909–1915 era. There are many pictures included, though none in color.

This book was intended to be a complete checklist book for collecting baseball cards, as there is space provided for checking off whether you have the card or not. As far as I know, this book is no longer available. This is a shame, for it contains a lot of valuable information.

Hobby Periodicals

The Old Publications

There have been many magazines, newspapers, newsletters, and other assorted periodicals published about baseball card collecting over the years. Jefferson Burdick started the first newsletter, *The Card Collector's Bulletin,* in the late 1930s. Some of the other periodicals that have come and gone over the years include *Sport Fan,* published by Bob Jaspersen from the early 1950s into the early 1980s; *Card Comments* from the early 1960s; and many from the 1970s, including *Sports Collectors News, The Sports Collecting World, The Sport Hobbyist, Sports Scoop,* and *The Trader Speaks.* None of these publications exist today, but they provided a valuable service to baseball card collectors of the past. Today there are many fine periodicals devoted to baseball card collecting and related sports collecting. Krause Publications owns three of the leaders, *Sports Collectors Digest, Sports Collectors News,* and *Baseball Cards Magazine.* Frank and Vivian Barning publish *Baseball Hobby News.* Others, including *Tuff Stuff, Beckett Baseball Card Monthly, The Old Judge,* and *The Wrapper,* cater to specific subgroups of card collectors.

The old baseball card publications were quite different from those that exist today. In general, the old publications were run by one individual who was a baseball card collector. In many cases, the publisher was a major advertiser and used the publication to make extra money selling cards. Many of the early publications did not have a professional look to them, and the paid circulation was usually very low, leading some to go out of business without notice. As a result, many longtime baseball card collectors are still wary when ordering subscriptions to hobby magazines.

The contents of these old baseball card periodicals generally consisted of articles, checklists of baseball card issues, feature ads, and classified advertising. The articles were often very interesting, with in-depth studies of specific card issues, information about new issues, and discussion of rarities and pricing information. For example, in the June 1973 issue of *Sports Collectors News,* there is an article and checklist for the 1968 Atlantic Oil baseball card set, including a list of cards that were redeemable for cash prizes. The Spring 1973 issue of *The Sport Hobbyist* contains an article about card shows around the country that says that the crowd of over 600 people at the Chicago convention of March 1973 probably set the all-time attendance record for a baseball card show.

In the years between the last update of *The American Card Catalog* and the first *Sport Americana Baseball Card Price Guide* there were many sets of baseball cards issued, but few sources of checklist information. There were baseball card checklists available from some baseball card dealers, but these generally listed only the major card sets issued after World War II. Collectors had to rely on the periodicals for checklist information on new issues, regionals, food inserts, and obscure sets. There were generally several different checklists in each issue of most of the old magazines.

There were always many ads, and advertising rates were very low. A full-page ad in *The Trader Speaks* in 1974 cost $40. A quarter-page ad in *Sports Collectors Digest (SCD)* in 1974 cost just $4 (By contrast, the price was up to $160 for a quarter-page ad in *SCD* in 1989.) Most of the ads were placed by collectors who wanted to trade or sell off their duplicates. The majority of the cards for sale were available through mail auctions. This was probably because there was no standard price guide before 1979, and the sellers were not really sure about what their cards were worth. In an issue of *The Trader Speaks* in 1974, there were 25 auction ads and only 6 sale ads. Classified ads were abundant, with a fairly even distribution of ''for sale,'' ''wanted,'' and ''trade'' ads.

In general, each issue of the older hobby publications contained from 10 to 40 pages. *The Trader Speaks* was the recognized leader in hobby publications through most of the 1970s,

with *Sports Collectors Digest* steadily gaining in popularity through the years. The September 20, 1974, issue of *Sports Collectors Digest* listed its circulation at 2,674. Most of the other publications declined to list their circulation figures.

Current Publications

There are a number of quality sports-collecting publications available today. Most of the current hobby papers are very professionally produced, with stable ownership and large circulations. The biggest hobby publications have been in business for many years. Addresses for the current hobby periodicals are listed in Appendix C of this book.

Krause Publications

The oldest and largest of the current baseball card magazines is *Sports Collectors Digest*. *SCD* was started in 1973 by John Stommen of Milan, Michigan, and it immediately created an impact in the hobby with its professional appearance and inexpensive subscription and ad rates. In the early years of *SCD*, its main competitor was *The Trader Speaks (TTS)*. The two publications battled head to head for subscription business through the years, with *SCD* continually gaining in popularity and *TTS* gradually declining.

In 1979, Krause Publications purchased *SCD* from Stommen and moved the publication site to Iola, Wisconsin. Krause Publications owns a long list of magazines concerning many different hobbies, including coins, stamps, and comic books. Under its new ownership, *SCD* has remained the leader in page length per issue, circulation, and number of issues

Fig. 4-11. Two of the premier baseball card hobby publications: Sports Collectors Digest *and* Baseball Hobby News.

per year. *SCD* is regularly over 200 pages in length, with a circulation of over 30,000, and is published weekly. In 1983, Krause publications bought the declining *TTS* and promptly stopped its production, making *SCD* the longest running sports hobby publication.

Over the years, *SCD* has become the main marketplace for mail-order baseball card collecting. Each issue contains mostly ads, with some news, a few articles, a convention calendar, and a baseball card price guide. Most of the display ads list cards and other collectibles that are for sale from baseball card dealers. There are also some auction and want ads, as well as an advertiser index. There is a large classified section with subheadings for specific types of ads.

In recent years, Krause Publications has increased its presence in the baseball card publication field by adding other hobby magazines. Krause purchased *Sports Collectors News* (a hobby magazine emphasizing articles a little more than *SCD*) from Allen Kaye of San Diego, the original owner. *Baseball Cards* magazine, which appears on magazine stands, began as a Krause publication and contains a full-color

cover and a few color pages in each monthly issue. In addition, two specialty magazines debuted in the summer of 1988: *Baseball Card Show Calendar* and *Baseball Card Price Guide Monthly*. *Baseball Card Show Calendar* is issued quarterly and contains extensive listings of upcoming baseball card shows. *Baseball Card Price Guide Monthly* contains extensive price listings for the major baseball card sets issued since 1948 (Fig. 4-11).

Baseball Hobby News

Frank and Vivian Barning have been putting out a quality magazine called *Baseball Hobby News (BHN)* since 1979. *BHN*, based in San Diego, California, provides articles for every level of collector and investor of baseball cards and memorabilia. *BHN* has separated itself from its competition by presenting editorial comments and analysis of hobby issues. *BHN* is not afraid to take a stand on an issue, and this often makes for interesting reading.

BHN employs a wide range of staff writers from around the United States that are highly regarded in specific fields of the sports-collecting hobby. For example, staff writer Ralph Nozaki is probably the most knowledgeable individual in the hobby on baseball card errors and variations. Staff writer Paul Wright has a great deal of knowledge about baseball card wrappers.

Another feature of *BHN* is a "Who's Who" section featuring write-ups on baseball card collectors. Anyone can appear in Who's Who by filling out and sending in a questionnaire from an issue of *BHN*. The Who's Who section gives collectors a chance to talk about what they collect, things they like about the hobby, and their hobby goals.

BHN also has a good deal of advertising, with many display ads and classifieds, as well as an advertiser index. A schedule of upcoming baseball card shows is also included.

Other Publications

Smaller publications that appeal to specific segments of the card-collecting hobby include *The Old Judge, Tuff Stuff, Beckett Baseball Card Monthly,* and *The Wrapper.*

The Old Judge is a newsletter put out by Lew Lipset of Centereach, New York. Lipset is an authority on nineteenth-century and early twentieth-century baseball cards. His newsletter specializes in those early cards.

Tuff Stuff is published by Ernie White of Richmond, Virginia. The recent emphasis of this monthly newspaper has been on minor league baseball cards. There are price guides for minor league sets, unopened material, football card sets, non-sports cards, and other items not found in other magazines. There is also a regular column about non-sports cards. *Tuff Stuff* attempts to fill gaps left by other publications.

Beckett Baseball Card Monthly is mainly a monthly price guide update to Beckett's annual *Sport Americana Baseball Card Price Guide.* There are also articles and other card information in each issue.

The Wrapper is put out by Les Davis of Carol Stream, Illinois. It is a publication devoted strictly to non-sports cards. *The Wrapper* resembles some of the early baseball card publications. There is considerably less money and interest in the non-sports segment of card collecting, so it is more difficult to get subscribers for a publication such as this. The subscription level in May 1989 was listed at 1,500. Still, this is a fun magazine that covers a segment of card collecting that is still extremely affordable for the collector.

Building a Collection

Collecting Goals

Many collectors set lofty goals for themselves when they start a baseball card collection. A common goal is "to collect one of every card ever made." Most collectors who set this goal soon realize that even if this goal were financially feasible (which is unlikely for most people), it may still be unattainable because of the lack of availability of some cards. Even the best collections in the world do not contain copies of all cards ever made. There are some cards that are so rare that only one or two are known. There are other cards that are rumored

to exist but have not been verified. There are still others that might have existed at one time, but do not exist anymore.

Because the initial goal of collecting one of every card ever issued is unfeasible, most collectors decide to collect only certain types of cards. There are many different types of baseball cards available, and it is much easier and more satisfying to concentrate your efforts on certain sets or types of cards, rather than trying to get everything.

Keeping Track of What's Available

In order to decide on what types of cards to collect, you have to know what's available. Once you know what's out there, you can decide on which cards you want and can develop a plan for getting them.

Keeping Track of Old Cards

The best source for finding out about old cards is a baseball card price guide. The price

guides contain complete checklists of all of the most popular baseball card sets. They also include sample pictures and pricing information for cards from each set. If you want to see *everything* that's available, get a copy of *The Standard Catalog of Baseball Cards* by Krause Publications. If you plan to specialize in cards from a certain team or cards of individual players, there are books to help you see what's available. *The Team Baseball Card Checklist*

Fig. 5-1. A 1987 Donruss rack pack.

and *The Baseball Card Alphabetical Checklist,* both available from Sport Americana, can provide some help.

Keeping Track of New Cards

It's a little bit more difficult to find out about new baseball card sets as they are being issued. The best way to find information on new sets is to subscribe to one of the baseball card hobby magazines. *Sports Collectors Digest, Baseball Hobby News, Sports Collectors News,* and *Baseball Cards Magazine* all announce the release of new baseball card issues either before or during their initial release period. (Addresses for these magazines can be found in Appendix C in the back of this book.) Each of these magazines usually reports just about every new set that's issued, though they occasionally miss one here and there.

Since the hobby magazines are not perfect, it's also important for you to keep your eyes and ears open for new sets. It takes a little luck to find out about some new sets, but if you know where to look, you can make the odds more in your favor. There are several types of stores where new issues of baseball cards are commonly found. These include drugstores, minimarts, grocery stores, toy

stores, sporting goods stores, and baseball stadium gift shops. Most baseball card sets are issued with gum, candy, or other food products. By continuously checking the candy counters at local drugstores and minimarts and keeping your eyes open when grocery shopping, you can sometimes find baseball card sets that the hobby periodicals miss. Some grocery store products that have used baseball cards as promotional items include popcorn, potato chips, bread, milk, soda pop, breakfast cereals, cookies, snack cakes, candy bars, ice cream, hot dogs, iced tea, and even dog food. Check several different stores if you can, because some baseball cards come with brand-specific products that aren't carried by every store. For example, Meadow Gold dairy products came with baseball cards in several parts of the country in 1986, and this brand could only be found at certain stores.

Toy stores are a good place to look for new baseball card issues. They often carry rack packs of the major baseball cards and sometimes have a good variety of different issues available (Fig. 5-1). There are also some baseball card products that are sold exclusively at toy stores. For example, Kenner has recently issued a set of baseball player statues with baseball cards through toy stores.

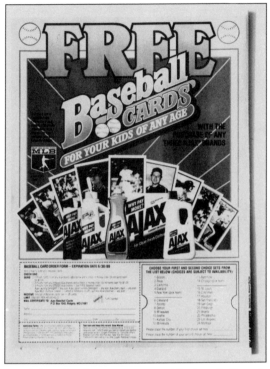

Fig. 5-2. A Sunday newspaper ad for baseball cards from Colgate-Palmolive Co. The ad offered free baseball cards through the mail with proof of purchase from Ajax products.

shop. The gift shops at the stadium often sell baseball card sets for the local team. While you are there, you can also pick up free team pocket schedules. These schedules are a collectible in themselves, and they also list games at which the team will give away free merchandise to fans in attendance. Check this listing, because many teams include free baseball cards as a promotional item at a game or two during the year.

Another place to look for new card issues is in the Sunday newspaper. In recent years, the Sunday paper has occasionally contained ads for mail-in cards that were not available in stores. The two best places to look in the Sunday newspaper are in the comics section and the coupon sections (Fig. 5-2).

The best time to look for new baseball card issues is during the spring and summer months, when the baseball season is in full swing. By occasionally checking the sources listed above, you can usually spot new baseball card issues as they come out.

Sporting goods stores are another place where baseball cards are sometimes found. For example, Louisville Slugger has been giving away baseball cards with baseball gloves for several years now. These cards are hard to obtain because the gloves usually cost $13 and up, and most people don't need new baseball gloves very often.

Another place to check for new baseball card issues is your local baseball stadium gift

Making a List

Because so many baseball card sets are coming out each year, it's sometimes hard to remember exactly what's available. That's why it's a good idea to keep a list of what is available or of what you want. Baseball card collectors have always kept checklists to keep track of what individual cards they need to complete a set, and now with so many new sets being issued it's becoming necessary to keep a checklist for the individual sets that are available.

Sources of Baseball Cards

There are a lot of different sources for obtaining baseball cards. Most people start their col-

lections by going down to a local dime store, drugstore, or minimarket and buying packs of

Fig. 5-3. Standard baseball card packs for 1988 Topps, 1988 Fleer, 1984 Donruss, and 1987 SportFlics cards.

cards. Packs of new cards generally cost in the 50-cent range for 15 cards. A nice collection can be built just from these purchases. However, to build a more thorough collection, other ways of obtaining cards must be used (Fig. 5-3).

Many new baseball card sets are produced every year. In recent years, over 100 new sets have been coming out each year, and there is every indication that there will be just as many sets issued in future years. It's hard to find some of these cards because they are regional issues and may not be available where you live. It's also very costly to buy every set issued each year. It is important to know where to look for cards and how much you will have to pay from various sources.

Once you know about the cards that are available, you need to develop a strategy for deciding which ones you want, how much you're willing to pay, and how to go about getting what you want for as little money as possible. You'll have to decide what you want,

but here are some of the places where you can find baseball cards, and the approximate prices you'll have to pay at each place.

Local Retail Stores

The new major issues of baseball cards can often be found at local candy stores, grocery stores, toy stores, and similar types of retail stores. You can also find new minor national issues and regional cards for your area at these stores. Most of these stores only carry one or two different types of cards at once, so you may have to go to different stores to find different brands.

When buying baseball cards at local retail stores, you will usually pay the exact suggested retail price for the cards. Some stores sell slightly below and some slightly above, but in most cases they sell cards for exact retail. Paying the retail price for baseball cards is usually reasonable.

For Topps baseball cards, you will usually

have to pay exact retail when you buy the cards by the pack no matter where you go, so local stores are as good a place as any to get them. If you want to buy in bulk—by the box or by the case—you can get a better price from other sources. In the past, you could sometimes find Topps cards with their prices slashed at the end of the baseball season, because the stores wanted to get rid of their excess supplies. In recent years, however, demand for baseball cards has been so high that there has been no excess supply and no sale prices at the end of the year.

For Donruss and Fleer baseball cards, the retail price was an excellent buy from 1984 to 1987 for Donruss and from 1986 to 1989 for Fleer. Unlike Topps, these companies did not produce enough cards to fill the demand for these years. Because of this, the cards were bought by hobby dealers and investors before they ever got to the shelves of local retail stores. Donruss has printed enough cards to satisfy demand since 1988, leading to lower prices for their cards and an abundant supply at retail stores. The supply of Fleer seems to be getting better, but if you see them on the shelf at a local store, the price you get will probably be better than any price you can get elsewhere.

For regional or national baseball cards that come with grocery products, prices vary depending on the cards themselves. These products get distributed in many different ways. Some of these sets wind up in the hands of baseball card dealers in great numbers, driving prices down; those sets that do not usually have very high prices. When dealers do acquire such cards in large numbers, it usually isn't until after the promotion ends, so it's hard to tell how many to buy while the promotion is still going. It's not easy to tell which sets will be abundant in the end and which will be scarce, but there are some general rules you can follow:

- If the set is produced by Topps for another company, there is a good chance that it will end up in large quantities with certain baseball card dealers. I don't know why this is true, but it may be that certain dealers have contacts with Topps employees or that the cards that remain after the promotion are sold to baseball card dealers at a low price. Examples of Topps-produced sets that are now held in large quantities by dealers are the Ralston Purina Cereal set of 1984, the Gardners Bread Brewers sets of 1984 and 1985, and the Quaker Chewy Granola set of 1986. (Note: This rule doesn't always work, as the 1984 Nestlé set is fairly scarce.)

- If the cards have to be cut off the box of a product, there's a good chance that they will be scarce in the future. This is because it is hard for dealers to acquire large numbers of cards that are cut off boxes. There have not been many cases of dealers getting unused boxes, so just about every card that is distributed goes to a person who actually buys the product. Examples include the Drakes Cake cards of 1986 to 1988, which are usually priced at $20 or more for a complete set; Drakes Cake sets distributed from 1981–1985 that were not cut off of boxes are usually priced at $5 to $8 for a set. Other examples include Hostess cards from 1975 to 1979 and Post Cereal cards from 1960 to 1963. Both of these issues are fairly scarce because few people own large quantities.

- If a set is only issued regionally, it is probably going to be scarcer than a set that is distributed nationally. If you are in the regional area of the set, buying the cards at a local retail store will probably be the cheapest way to get the cards. Even though regional cards are scarcer than national issues, collector demand is lower, so take that into consideration before investing your life savings into these cards. For example, the 1986 Keller's

Fig. 5-4. The packaging for food products containing baseball cards often features colorful advertising. Pictured are packages for Granny Goose potato chips cards from 1983, Jiffy Pop popcorn cards from 1986, Quaker Chewy Granola Bar cards from 1986, and Kellogg's Sugar Corn Pops cards from 1983.

butter Phillies set is a very scarce regional, but there is not much demand for it so its value remains fairly low.

• Some cards come with a mail-in offer for the entire set. These cards will generally be found in greater quantities than cards that don't have a mail-in offer. Also, it is usually cheaper to use the mail-in offer to get the cards than to buy the product to get them. For example, in the 1970s and early 1980s Kellogg annually put out a set of 3-D baseball cards with its cereal. You could get one card in each box of cereal, but you could get the entire set of 50 to 75 cards by sending in $2 to $3 and two box tops (Fig. 5-4).

Baseball Stadiums

Probably half of the major league teams now have an annual baseball card giveaway game each season or other promotions involving baseball cards. The giveaways usually involve a small set of cards featuring players from the home team, available only to fans attending the game. For sets of cards that are given out at the ballpark, it is almost always cheaper to get the cards at the ballpark than to get them from other sources. Good examples are the Mother's Cookies cards that have been given out at various ballparks in recent years. For example, you could get the Mother's Padres sets in 1984 and 1985 for $3 with a general admission ticket to the giveaway game; dealers later priced the sets from $10 to $20 each.

Baseball Card Stores

A fairly new way to get cards is to go to a baseball card store. The first baseball card stores opened in the late 1970s, and there are now baseball card stores in most major cities and in many smaller cities as well. Most baseball card stores offer a variety of new and old cards, from unopened material to complete sets and individual cards.

Most baseball card stores carry every brand of the current major issues. This saves you the trouble of having to go to many different stores to look for baseball cards. In addition, you usually have the choice of buying the cards in unopened packs or in complete sets. Buying them in complete sets saves you the trouble of having to build a set from scratch. It also deprives you of the fun of assembling a set yourself, so you'll have to decide which approach you prefer.

Prices for new cards are usually set at the retail rate or higher for unopened material and at price guide rates for opened material. Most new unopened material is sold at retail prices, but some hard-to-find packs are sold at higher rates. For example, most baseball card stores carried the 1989 Fleer cards, but sold them for considerably more than their retail price of 45 cents a pack. The 1989 Fleer cards were rarely seen in retail stores.

Baseball card stores also offer you a good place to get older cards. Most baseball card stores stock a wide range of older baseball cards, from singles to complete sets. It is often possible to get singles of common players from older sets at stores. Stores wll carry these cards, but dealers usually will not bring them to baseball card shows because display space is lacking and the profit margin is too small.

Stores offer you the convenience of being able to take a look around before buying. You can usually take your time more than you can at a baseball card show, because there are generally fewer people milling around at a baseball card store. Baseball card stores will not offer you the same selection of cards or the price competition that shows provide, however.

Baseball card stores offer you an advantage over mail order in that you can see what you're buying, you can get the cards immediately, and you don't have to pay postage costs. You don't have to worry about the condition of the cards being lower than you expect, since you can examine them before you buy. Some baseball card stores will give you a price discount if you place a large order. It's harder to bargain for a discount through the mail.

Baseball card stores are also an excellent place to get supplies. Stores usually carry plastic pages, binders, storage boxes, hobby publications, price guides, and other items to help you with your collecting.

To locate baseball card stores in your area, check the Yellow Pages under "Baseball Cards" or "Collectibles." Quite often, baseball card stores will be listed under these headings. There is an "Announcement" category in the classified ads section of *Sports Collectors Digest* where some baseball card stores advertise and provide location information. You might want to check this for stores in your area. *The Baseball Card Dealer Directory,* available from Meckler books, contains a comprehensive listing of baseball card dealers around the country.

Baseball Card Shows

Baseball card shows provide a good way to buy cards at competitive prices. There are usually many dealers that are selling the same cards, which leads to competition. Prices for cards at shows are usually lower than you can find at stores. Shows also give you the advantage of being able to buy from a lot of different sellers who are all offering somewhat different material. For example, one dealer might sell the major sets, while another might have many different regional cards from all over the country. The main disadvantages of shows are that you usually have to pay an admission fee to enter and they are usually only convenient when they happen to take place in your area.

Baseball cards are sold in a number of different ways at shows. For older cards, some dealers offer bulk lots, which enable you to buy a large group of cards for one price. If bulk lots are advertised as "different" cards, you know that all of the cards will be different (no duplicates). If bulk lots are advertised as "assorted" cards, the cards are not necessarily all different; in fact, there are probably duplicates within the lot. Some bulk lots are sold with star players, some without stars. The cost per card is usually less when you buy in bulk lots than when you buy the cards individually. If you need most or all of the cards in a particular set, it is usually a good idea to start collecting that set by first buying bulk lots.

Many baseball card dealers sell single cards of star players. The prices for these will vary greatly depending on card condition and on the dealer. Take care to learn the price guide value for older cards before buying them, and be sure to shop around before making a buying decision. There will often be widely varying prices for the same cards from different dealers at a baseball card show, so take your time and try to get the best deal you can.

Listings of baseball card shows by region of the country appear in some of the hobby magazines. These listings usually tell you where shows in your area are being held, along with the admission fee and the dealer fee. You can also often find out about local baseball card shows from ads in the sports section of your local newspaper. When you go to a show, the promoters often want you to fill in your name and address for their mailing list. Be sure to do so, for you will automatically be informed by mail about future shows.

Buying Through Mail Order

The baseball card magazines are all loaded with advertisements from mail-order baseball card dealers. There is usually a wide variety of material for sale, from unopened boxes, cases, and complete sets of new cards to singles, bulk lots, and complete sets of older cards. If you continue to watch the magazine ads over a period of time, you will have the opportunity to buy just about any baseball card that has ever been made. Even the most valuable baseball cards such as the T206 Honus Wagner and the 1933 Goudey Nap Lajoie have been advertised in recent years in the baseball card magazines.

You can usually get a very good price on new cards from some mail-order advertisers. You have to go through the ads and compare prices to get the best deal, and you also have to add any applicable postage costs to your price totals to see if buying through the mail is worthwhile. You can usually obtain cards in just about any quantity through mail order, and most baseball card dealers are very reliable and fast when sending out orders. Many dealers will delay sending an order paid for by personal check until the check clears, but a large percentage of dealers offer one-day service for money orders. Many of the larger dealers now accept major credit cards.

The hobby magazines not only have ads from dealers offering to sell cards, but they also have auction ads. Baseball card auctions sometimes list minimum bids and sometimes don't. Auctions are often a great way to get cards inexpensively. When bidding in an auction with no minimum bid, bid only as much as you want to pay. People selling cards by auction are often prepared to accept bids that are less than the price guide value. Do not bother placing ridiculously low bids, because the usual rules in baseball card auctions do not require the advertiser to accept the highest bid— they only require the advertiser to accept the highest *reasonable* bid. Therefore, if you are the only bidder for a 1952 Topps Mickey Mantle card at $10, it would be very surprising if you got the card.

There are a lot of good points about ordering baseball cards through the mail. You can shop and compare prices in the privacy of your own home and at your convenience. The prices are usually competitive, and you can find cards that are issued in just about any region of the country. There are also a couple of disadvantages to ordering through the mail. You will usually have to wait from one week to two or three months for your order, depending on the dealer and whether the cards are in stock. In some cases, especially in recent years, dealers will not honor their advertised prices for new cards if the cards you order prove to be hot and are rising in price quickly. This has been especially true for Donruss and Fleer cards in recent years and for some of the Update and Traded sets that come out at the end of the year. Although these cases are rare, cards you order could get lost or damaged in the mail or the dealer could take your money and send you back nothing in return. Fortunately, most dealers send their orders by United Parcel Service (UPS), and this usually protects you from lost or damaged cards because UPS automatically insures all packages to a certain

value. Also, there have been very few cases of advertisers swindling money from mail-in buyers, and when this does happen the hobby papers have been quick to blacklist the responsible individuals from advertising in the magazines in the future.

In general, it's fairly safe and easy to order baseball cards through mail-order dealers. It's also fun to get a package of baseball cards delivered to your door in the mail.

Classified Ads

Placing classified ads is sometimes a good way to get baseball cards. You can place an ad in one of the baseball card hobby magazines or in a local paper in your area.

There are a lot of baseball card dealers who place huge ads in baseball card magazines offering to buy cards at high prices. You probably won't get a very good response to a classified ad that tries to compete with these dealers. You may get a better response if you advertise to buy specific baseball cards or cards from specific sets. Classified ads in hobby papers are sometimes very helpful in locating the last card you need to complete a set or for obtaining cards of a specific player or team.

Placing a classified ad in a local paper sometimes works very well for locating cards. When advertising in a local paper, you won't be advertising to baseball card collectors only, but rather to anyone who reads the local paper. Some of the people who respond may have old collections that they're not interested in keeping. You can sometimes get nice collections at bargain prices. In the past, I achieved great results by simply placing small classified ads in local advertising publications. The cost is usually between $10 and $20 to place an ad, and it can usually be done over the phone.

Classified ads can be simple, stating something like:

Old baseball cards wanted. Will pay cash. Phone _____ .

Or they can be more specific, such as:

Jiffy Pop baseball cards wanted. Will pay 25¢ each. Phone _____ .

When you place a classified ad in a local paper, be sure to be home on the day the ad appears. Some people will call on a whim and will not call again if there is no answer. If you get a caller that sounds like he or she has some cards you want, set up an appointment to meet with the caller on another day to look at the cards.

Classified ads are a good thing to try if you're looking for new sources of cards. If you placed an ad in a local paper 10 years ago, the phone would be ringing off the hook for most of the day with people looking to sell their cards at reasonable prices. It's getting more difficult to get good deals using classifieds these days, as baseball card interest has risen in recent years.

Using advertising in another similar way, some collectors have rented rooms at local hotels and then advertised for people to come and sell the collectors their cards. Recently some card dealers did this in Venezuela and uncovered many cards that were issued by Topps in Spanish versions with different coloring than their regular United States versions. Since these cards are almost never seen in the United States, they were quite a find.

Flea Markets, Swap Meets, and Antique Stores

Flea markets, swap meets, and antique stores offer you the chance to find baseball cards for bargain prices. The people who are selling items at these places do not usually specialize in baseball cards. Because of this, you may be able to get a good deal if you find some cards for sale. On the other hand, some of these dealers overprice their cards because of their lack of knowledge of their true values.

Searching flea markets, swap meets, and antique stores for baseball cards can be a time-consuming proposition. It is likely that you will have to go through the materials of many dealers before finding any cards. Still, you do have the potential to find interesting items that have not been discovered by others in the baseball card hobby.

Friends and Relatives

Friends and relatives are among the best sources for getting baseball cards. It's important to spread the word that you're a collector. Some people consider baseball card collecting to be a hobby just for kids, and a lot of collectors are embarrassed to tell people about their collections. If you can get over this embarrassment and tell people that you collect, you will often discover unknown sources for cards. There are a lot of people out there who collected cards as a kid and still have the cards stashed away somewhere. If you let them know of your interest in cards, they will sometimes give you their cards for free or for a very reasonable price.

Friends and relatives have always been a great source of baseball cards for me. An aunt who knew I collected cards once gave me a nice group of baseball coins from the early 1960s as a Christmas present. Her son had collected baseball cards and baseball coins from the late 1950s and early 1960s. He wanted to keep his cards, but he let her give the coins to me. This was a great gift and gave me my first real start in collecting these items. I never would

Fig. 5-5. Baseball coins: 1962 Salada Don Schwall, 1963 Salada Warren Spahn, 1964 Topps Ray Culp, 1988 Topps Bobby Bonilla. Topps coins copyright The Topps Company, Inc.

have gotten them if I had kept quiet about my collection (Fig. 5-5).

In recent years my relatives from around the country have been helping me get some of the regional cards that I can't get in my area. I'll let them know when a new card set is issued in their area, and they can usually pick me up a set. This is almost always less expensive than going through a baseball card dealer.

Trading

Trading baseball cards is a time-honored tradition. Almost every kid that collects baseball cards has traded with friends. Some of the shrewdest business people of today learned how to put together deals through the baseball card trading experiences of their youths. Many old-time collectors would not sell their most valuable duplicates, as they saved them for trading.

It seems as if trading is being done less and less these days, even though it is easier than ever to do. Because of price guides, it is relatively simple to compare the prices for different cards and make fair trade proposals. For example, if you have a group of cards from the mid-1970s to trade for some cards from the mid-1960s, you can figure out a fair trade just by adding up the values for the cards from a price guide. Price guides take into consideration all the factors of the cards, such as condition, star players, and high numbers. Before

price guides were available, figuring out fair trades was very difficult.

It may be that because of the price guides, prices for cards have become higher and more volatile, making people more wary of trades for fear of getting the worst of a deal. Also, with the advent of more baseball card dealers, there are more people involved in baseball cards for the money these days. Dealers are usually unwilling to make trades unless they clearly get the better end of the deal. Since most collectors don't want to get the worst of a deal when trading with a dealer, trades between collectors and dealers are rare.

Still, it's possible to do some trading in today's baseball card world. These days, trading is done primarily to save money. Since you can buy almost every baseball card set that is issued today through baseball card dealers, trading is not usually done because it is the only way to get certain cards. Instead, smart collectors will stockpile cards that they can get cheaply or that are only available in their area and use their extra cards to trade for cards that aren't so readily available.

The 1987 baseball cards offered a great opportunity for trading. In 1987, the distribution of the major baseball card sets varied in different regions of the country. People in the eastern part of the United States seemed to have an easier time getting cards that were made by Fleer, and people in the western half of the country had an easier time getting Donruss cards. Because of this, some people in the

West traded their Donruss cards to people in the East for Fleer cards.

Some collectors around the country have been accumulating large quantities of regional issues from their areas and using them to trade for regionals from other parts of the country. For example, regionals that are issued at the ballpark on baseball card day will usually cost you the price of the cheapest admission to the park, usually $3 to $5. By buying several admissions or getting all of your friends to go to the game and getting their cards, you can build up a supply of those cards. They can be used to trade for regional sets from other parts of the country that might cost quite a bit from a baseball card dealer.

Other ways of accumulating tradable cards might be to eat certain food products that are sold with cards and to get all of your friends to help by saving their cards for you. You can also start a mini business by selling the food products that come with cards to others and keeping the cards for yourself. For example, I did this in the late 1980s with the Quaker Chewy Granola Bar set and the Nestlé chocolate cards. I sold the candy bars at cost at my workplace and kept the cards for myself. Everybody won because the people at work enjoyed the snack bars and I was able to accumulate extra cards. By the time the promotions ended, I had put together a lot of extra sets. I then made some trades to acquire sets from around the country that I couldn't get in my area.

Trading sometimes allows you to take advantage of the fluctuating market for baseball cards in a better way than buying and selling do. You can use the hot cards of the moment to trade for some older, more stable cards. For example, in 1981 there was a big demand for a Fleer error card of Graig Nettles with his name misspelled *Craig Nettles* on the back. I managed to get a few duplicates of this card from my Fleer purchases that year. The value of the card quickly shot up to about $10 in the summer of 1981. I placed a classified ad offering to trade this card for some superstar cards of the late 1950s and early 1960s that were valued at about $10 each. As a result, I made three trades that brought the cards I needed. I only spent about 6 cents for the three cards I traded and got cards that would have cost me $30. Since 1981, the value for the C. Nettles card has remained at about $10, but the interest is much lower. I probably couldn't have made those trades today. When an obscenity was discovered on the 1989 Fleer Bill Ripken card and a huge rush of publicity followed, other people made similar trades of that card to obtain older cards with more stable values.

When you have some trading material and you want to make a trade, you have to find a trading partner. The best way to locate someone is to check the classified ads in the hobby papers. Often people from other parts of the country will have the same idea and will place ads looking for trading partners. If you don't see enough of these ads, it only costs a few dollars to place your own classified ad in the hobby papers, and the response is usually very good. Also, you might want to check the display ads, because some card dealers will trade a wide assortment of sets for a quantity of a set they need. Though it might take some creativity and initiative, trading is still a fun and inexpensive way to get new cards for your collection.

Candy Distributors

If you want to buy baseball cards in bulk, usually by the box or by the case, you can sometimes get a good deal from a local candy distributor. The baseball card manufacturers sell their wax pack cases directly to candy distributors around the country. The intention of the manufacturers is that these distributors will sell the cards at wholesale prices to local retail stores.

Some of the major baseball card manufacturers do not sell their wax pack products directly to baseball card dealers, but only to candy distributors. Through 1989, this policy was still being maintained for Topps and Fleer cards, though Score, SportFlics, and Upper Deck sealed pack cases could be purchased directly by baseball card dealers.

If you wish to buy boxes and cases of cards from candy distributors, you need to obtain the necessary permits for your area to become a seller of merchandise, but these are usually free and fairly easy to obtain. Once you have the required permits, you are free to call up any candy distributors in your area and buy cards directly from them. You can find these distributors in the yellow pages under the "Candy Distributors" heading.

A lot of baseball card dealers have been buying cards in this way in the past few years, and candy distributors are now sometimes charging higher-than-wholesale prices for baseball cards. Some distributors are also selling out of cards very quickly. It was reported in the hobby papers that one baseball card dealer even went so far as to send letters to every candy distributor in the United States, offering to buy 1987 Donruss cases at full retail price instead of the wholesale price that the cards are usually sold for by distributors.

In recent years, many baseball card dealers have been complaining that they cannot get wax cases of cards directly from the manufacturers. They feel that it is unfair for them to have to go through candy distributors to get these products. One of the main reasons for the absence of some brands of baseball cards from retail stores is that the cards that are intended for those stores are purchased by baseball card dealers instead.

Card Manufacturers (Direct)

Another way of getting baseball cards in bulk is to get them directly from the baseball card manufacturers. Topps, Fleer, Donruss, Major League Marketing, and Upper Deck all sell baseball cards directly to baseball card hobby dealers. There is usually a minimum order requirement of at least five cases, so the investment is usually at least a thousand dollars. The major card manufacturers all require you to send them a copy of your seller's permit before they will send you any ordering information. Donruss requires you to fill out a questionnaire before it will put you on its Donruss Dealer Network.

Topps produces different products for different distribution channels. Baseball card dealers who order directly from Topps can only buy cards from the regular set in vending cases. These cases consist of 24 boxes of cards, each box containing 500 randomly assorted cards. There is no gum and the cards are not packed in wax packs or in any other packaging. (Topps does not sell wax packs, rack packs, cello packs, or any other type of packaged cards from its regular set to baseball card dealers.) Topps also sells its year-end Traded set directly to dealers. These cards are sold as complete sets and are distributed only through baseball card dealers. In the past, Topps has set a minimum order of five cases of cards for baseball hobby dealers. Unlike Fleer or Donruss, Topps allows reorders throughout the year. Topps also has a policy of not selling any baseball cards from past seasons—the company will only sell its current product.

Fleer sells its regular card set directly to baseball hobby dealers in complete sets. Fleer packages a number of complete sets per case and sets a minimum order of five cases. In recent years, Fleer has been honoring all orders placed before a certain date, but the com-

Fig. 5-6. A box containing a complete set of 1988 Score baseball cards. The manufacturer sold these cards directly to card dealers in cases of complete sets.

pany has not been accepting reorders. It also has not always told dealers when the cutoff date for orders will be for a given year, forcing dealers to get their orders in very early in order to reserve some cards. Fleer has also been producing a year-end update set that is sold only through baseball hobby dealers.

Baseball card dealers on the Donruss Dealer Network have been receiving a letter with their allotment of cards for a particular issue. They then have the choice of ordering part or all of their allotment, and they can request more cards if the cards are available. The allotments that have been given to baseball card dealers have sometimes been much smaller than many dealers would like. For example, in 1987 most small baseball card dealers and dealers who were placing their first orders received an allotment of only two cases of Donruss complete sets. There is no reorder policy with Donruss at the present time, meaning that the allotment that is given to dealers before the baseball season is the total amount of cards that the dealers can order. Donruss has been known to blacklist dealers that decide not to order less popular items. Blacklisted dealers are not sent future offerings of more popular items.

Donruss had been selling only complete sets to dealers, but in 1987 it began selling cases of wax packs directly to baseball card dealers as well. This may have been in response to attempts by a few baseball card dealers to corner the market on Donruss wax pack products.

Major League Marketing and Upper Deck have been selling their cards directly to dealers in cases of complete sets and in cases of sealed packages. They both set minimum order levels, and Major League Marketing has been accepting reorders on its Score and SportFlics cards (Fig. 5-6).

A Few Last Words about Obtaining Cards

There are a few things you should keep in mind when you are trying to obtain baseball cards for your collection:

• Always be prepared to walk away from a baseball card purchase if the price is too high. Even if you are trying to buy very rare cards, they will almost always be available again from another source. As an example, even the T206 Honus Wagner has been offered for sale many times in recent years through mail auctions in the hobby papers.

- Be patient but persistent. Do not be in too big of a hurry to get what you want. If you take your time and are persistent, you can obtain almost every card you want at a reasonable price. Many collectors buy the first card they see at a card show, only to see the card later at another dealer table for a lower price. Take your time, and this won't happen to you.

- Be creative. You don't have to buy every card you want at dealer prices. For example, you might want to stockpile cards that you can get cheaply and trade them for ones that are more expensive or sell them and use the profits to buy the more expensive cards.

If you keep these thoughts in mind, it will be much easier and less costly for you to go about the process of building a baseball card collection.

Using Price Guides to Follow the Market

A lot of people these days are investing money in baseball cards. While just about all baseball cards of the past have historically been good investments, this may not necessarily hold true for the future. There are much larger quantities of cards being produced today than even a few years ago. Unlike in the past, many of the cards bought these days are being hoarded and stored away for investment purposes. Of course, when the supply of a card set gets too high, the value of the cards will go down. It is important to be careful when investing in baseball cards today.

As with most investment situations, if we could see into the future it would be easy to figure out what baseball cards to invest in today. Since this is impossible, the next best thing is to look into the past and view trends in prices over the years. Understanding the past makes it easier to predict the future.

Charting Various Sets and Cards

The values listed here to chart the price trends of card sets and individual cards are taken from the 1960 *American Card Catalog,* the 1975 *Sports Collectors Bible,* the 1981, 1983, and 1985 editions of *Sport Americana Baseball Card Price Guide,* and the 1987 and 1989 editions of *Sports Collectors Digest Baseball Card Price Guide.* Prices listed are for mint or near-mint condition cards. Values for lesser condition cards will usually be *much* lower. The sets that are charted here are presented because they are good representations of some of the most popular baseball card sets issued over a long period of time and because they contain some cards of interest to price watchers.

N172 Old Judge

Issued from 1887 to 1890, the N172 Old Judge set was the first major baseball card set ever issued. Every card from this set is rare. Few cards in N172 have a significantly greater value because of scarcity, since all are considered to be scarce. There were several different cards issued for most players found in N172. Table 6-1 shows how the price guides have

Table 6-1. Price Guide Value Estimates for the N172 Old Judge Card Set

	1960	1975	1981	1983	1985	1987	1989
Common players	25¢	$2–$10	NA*	$25	NA	$50	$65
Cap Anson	NA	NA	NA	$200	NA	$550	$750
Connie Mack	NA	NA	NA	$200	NA	$400	$550
Ed Delahanty	NA	NA	NA	$110	NA	$250	$375

*NA = not available

estimated the value of the N172 cards over the years.

As you can see from Table 6-1, common cards from N172 rose in value by 2,400 percent in the 12 years from 1975 to 1987. Cards of all players doubled in value from 1983 to 1987 and continued to rise in 1989.

Cards of Hall of Fame players such as Cap Anson, Connie Mack, Ed Delahanty, and others did not sell for significantly more than the common player level in 1960 and 1975 and were not listed separately in *The American Card Catalog* or *The Sports Collectors Bible*. The 1981 and 1985 editions of *The Sport Americana Baseball Card Price Guide* did not carry values for N172 cards.

Cap Anson was probably the greatest player of the nineteenth century, and Anson card values have been reflecting this more and more through the years. Cards for Anson are found in other nineteenth-century sets, and all are priced far above cards of lesser players.

The N172 cards of Connie Mack are the only cards that were issued during his playing days. Mack retired after the 1896 season with a mediocre .245 lifetime batting average over 11 years. He later became famous as a baseball executive, managing the Philadelphia Athletics from the beginning of their existence in 1901 through 1950, by far the longest tenure

of any major league manager. Since he also owned the Athletics, he had more job security than most managers. In baseball today, there is a rule prohibiting the owners of a major league team from also managing it, but in Mack's day there was no such rule. Connie Mack was elected to the Hall of Fame in 1937.

The prices for Ed Delahanty's cards are listed to show the average value for most of the Hall of Famers in the N172 set. Delahanty was the best of five brothers who played in the majors near the turn of the century. His .345 lifetime batting average is the fourth highest total of all time. He was still in the prime of his career in 1903 when he died after falling from a railroad bridge in Niagara Falls, New York. He was allegedly kicked off of the team train because of drunkenness and tried to follow on foot. He apparently fell from the bridge during the darkness of night. Delahanty was elected to the Hall of Fame in 1945.

The T206 Tobacco Set

Issued from 1909 to 1911, the T206 tobacco set is still one of the most popular and highly collected sets of all time. There are several rare cards in this set, as well as an abundance of Hall of Fame players, many of whom are found in more than one pose. Table 6-2

Table 6-2. Price Guide Value Estimates for T206 Cards

	1960	1975	1981	1983	1985	1987	1989
Common players	10¢	50¢–$1	$4.50	$6	$8.50	$15	$50
Honus Wagner	$50	$1,500+	$15,000	$19,000	$25,000	$34,000	$95,000
Ed Plank	$10	$550	$5,000	$5,500	$5,500	$7,000	$9,000
Ty Cobb	NA*	NA	$90–$150	$110–$150	$160–$250	$300–$450	$1,200
Home Run Baker	NA	NA	$16	$18	$25	$36	$175

*NA = not available

shows how the price guides have estimated the value of the T206 cards over the years.

Common cards from T206 rose in value by almost 10,000 percent in the 14 years from 1975 to 1989. The rare Honus Wagner card rose from a value of $1,500 in 1975 to $95,000 in 1989.

The reasons for the high values of the Honus Wagner and Ed Plank cards were discussed in detail earlier in this book (see Chapter 2). Cards of Hall of Fame players such as Ty Cobb, Home Run Baker, and others did not sell for significantly more than the common player level in 1960 and 1975 and were not listed separately in *The American Card Catalog* or *The Sports Collectors Bible* (Fig. 6-1).

There were several different cards issued for some players in T206, including four different poses for Ty Cobb. Certain poses are worth slightly more than others due to scarcity. Cobb was one of the greatest players of all time, maybe the greatest, and his card prices have been rising rapidly over the past few years. Until recently, cards of Cobb sold for fairly low prices because they have always been relatively abundant. T206 cards were so popular when they were originally released that thousands have survived to the present. There are

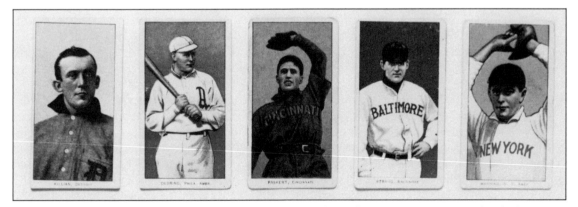

Fig. 6-1. T206 cards featuring Ed Killian, Rube Oldring, Dode Paskert, Sammy Strang, and Rube Manning.

Table 6-3. Price Guide Value Estimates for 1933 Goudey Cards

	1960	1975	1981	1983	1985	1987	1989
Common players	20¢	$1.50–$3	$8	$8.25	$12	$20	$45
Nap Lajoie	$1	$300	$6,000	$6,250	$6,000	$7,000	$15,000
Babe Ruth	NA*	$20+	$250–$275	$225–$275	$300–$375	$550–$700	$3,100
Lou Gehrig	NA	NA	$160	$160	$200	$450	$1,800
Lloyd Waner	NA	NA	$15	$14.50	$18	$32	$85

*NA = not available

more T206 cards available within the baseball card hobby than there are of probably any cards issued before the Bowman and Topps sets of the late 1940s and early 1950s.

The values for the card of Home Run Baker are listed to show the value for an average Hall of Famer in the T206 set. Home Run Baker got his famous nickname by hitting two home runs in the 1911 World Series. Baker played in the dead ball era of baseball, the era from the 1870s through 1919. The baseballs used in those years were softer and did not travel as far as those that were used after 1919 and up to the present time. Because of the "dead ball" it was much more difficult to hit a home run before 1920 than it would be in later years. The league leaders usually hit well under 20 homers for a season. Baker led the American League in home runs each year from 1911 through 1914, with his highest total being 12. He was elected to the Hall of Fame in 1955.

1933 Goudey

Also known as R319, the 1933 Goudey set is very historic because it was the first mass-produced baseball card set issued with bubble gum. Though there had been some small and relatively obscure sets of cards issued with chewing gum in the past, these were the first

to be issued in the manner that is familiar to collectors today. Goudey issued its cards in colorful wax wrappers along with a slab of bubble gum. Card #106 was missing in 1933, leading some to believe that it was left out on purpose so as to get collectors to buy more cards in the hopes of finding the missing number. Goudey eventually printed #106 in 1934, a card depicting Nap Lajoie, and released it in very small quantities. Table 6-3 shows how the price guides have estimated the value of the 1933 Goudey cards over the years.

The high value for the Nap Lajoie card is based almost entirely on its scarcity. The card was issued in minuscule numbers in comparison with the rest of the cards from this set. Since it wasn't ever issued with the rest of the 1933 Goudey cards, it really shouldn't be considered a part of the set. However, most collectors do consider it a part of the set because it contains the number 106 and because there isn't a better place to put it.

There are four different Babe Ruth cards, and they are no more scarce than any other card. In fact, #144 of Babe Ruth was double-printed, making it the most common card in the set. The second #144 card was printed in place of card #106. The high value of the Babe Ruth cards is entirely because of his standing as one of the greatest baseball players of all

Table 6-4. Price Guide Value Estimates for 1952 Topps Cards

	1960	1975	1981	1983	1985	1987	1989
Common players	10¢	50¢–$1.50	$2.75	$2.50	$3.50	$8	$20
Common players, #311–#407	30¢	$7–$11	$40	$32	$52	$95	$150
Mickey Mantle	NA*	NA	$1,500	$700	$2,100	$3,300	$6,500

*NA = not available

time. Babe Ruth changed the game of baseball from a scrappy, singles-hitting, base-stealing game into a home run game. His 54 home runs in 1920 were more than any other *team* in the American League hit that year. He retired with the record for most home runs in a season (60) and most home runs in a lifetime (714). He also compiled a lifetime batting average of .342 and a 94–46 won–lost record as a pitcher in his early years. Though he has since relinquished his single-season home run record to Roger Maris and his lifetime home run record to Hank Aaron, Babe Ruth's status as one of the greatest players of all time has not been diminished. Babe Ruth was elected to the Hall of Fame in 1936 as a member of the first group of five players ever selected.

The two cards of Lou Gehrig in the 1933 Goudey set are also valued highly because of Gehrig's standing as another of the all-time greats (not because of any scarcity). Gehrig was Ruth's teammate on the Yankees for many years and together with Ruth was largely responsible for making the Yankees a baseball dynasty. Gehrig holds the record for appearing in 2,130 consecutive games, a record that nobody has yet come close to equaling. He hit 493 lifetime home runs, leading the league three times, and compiled a .340 lifetime batting average. Gehrig was elected to the Hall of Fame in 1939.

The values for Lloyd Waner's card are listed to show the value for an average Hall of Famer in the 1933 Goudey set. Lloyd Waner was known as Little Poison, while his brother Paul, another Hall of Famer, was known as Big Poison. They starred together for many years in the outfield of the Pittsburgh Pirates, including the entire decade of the 1930s. Paul Waner also has a card in the 1933 Goudey set, which has about the same value as that of Lloyd. Paul compiled a lifetime batting average of .333, while Lloyd batted .316. Paul Waner was elected to the Hall of Fame in 1952 and Lloyd Waner joined him there in 1967.

1952 Topps

The 1952 issue was the first full-scale Topps baseball card set. Topps had released five small sets of cards in 1951 and a few baseball cards mixed in with other subjects in earlier card sets, but the 1952 cards represented the company's first major effort. A total of 407 numbered cards was issued, in several different series. The last series of cards, numbers 311 to 407, were distributed late in the year and in much smaller quantities than the rest of the cards in the set. Table 6-4 shows how the price guides have estimated the value of 1952 Topps cards over the years.

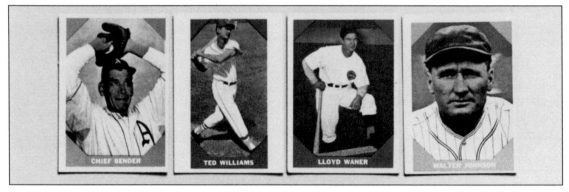

Fig. 6-2. 1960 Fleer Baseball Greats cards. Pictured are Chief Bender, Ted Williams, Lloyd Waner, and Walter Johnson. Williams was the only active player in the set at the time of issue.

All of the cards from this set have been rising steadily in value over the years. This set has proved to be one of the most popular sets for collectors, as the cards are very colorful and well-designed.

Card #311 of Mickey Mantle has become the most valuable baseball card issued since the Second World War. This card is a part of the scarce high-numbered series, but it was double-printed, making it one of the most abundant high-numbered cards issued. It is the first Mantle card issued by Topps, though it is not the first card of Mantle, as Bowman included him in its 1951 set. Interestingly, the 1952 Topps Mantle bears the distinction of being the first baseball card to ever take a big drop in value. After reaching a $1,500 value in 1981, it took a severe nosedive to $700 in 1983 before recovering and climbing to $6,500 in 1989.

Mickey Mantle was a great Yankee outfielder who hit 536 lifetime home runs and set a record with 18 World Series homers. He was always a popular player, and his popularity has carried over to the baseball card hobby. At the present time, he seems to be the most popular retired player for baseball card collectors and investors. Mickey Mantle was elected to the Hall of Fame in 1974.

1960 Fleer Baseball Greats

The 1960 Fleer Baseball Greats set shows that some baseball card sets have not risen as dramatically in price as others. In 1960, as in later years, Fleer was prevented from producing a set of baseball cards of current players because Topps had exclusive agreements with almost every player. Instead of picturing active players, Fleer released a set of great retired players. Every player in the set was retired except for Ted Williams, whom Fleer had under exclusive contract. (Williams was not pictured in Topps sets of 1959 and 1960 because of his agreement with Fleer.) (Fig. 6-2.)

Traditionally, sets depicting players who are retired at the time of issue have not generated much collector interest. Collectors consider cards of active players (at time of issue) to be much more desirable than cards of retired players, probably because the collector has the sense of owning a part of history when the card pictures an active player.

Table 6-5 shows price guide values for 1960 Fleer cards over the years. Though the cards from this set have risen in value over the years, the increases are not nearly as dramatic as in most card sets. While T206 common cards were

Table 6-5. Price Guide Value Estimates for 1960 Fleer Cards

	1975	1981	1983	1985	1987	1989
Common players	15¢–50¢	40¢	47¢	60¢	60¢	$1.00
Babe Ruth	NA*	$4.00	$5.50	$7.50	$7.50	$25.00
Ted Williams	NA	$2.50	$4.25	$5.50	$7.00	$15.00
Complete set	$15.00	$45.00	$55.00	$66.00	$125.00	$170.00

*NA = not available

Table 6-6. Price Guide Value Estimates for 1963 Topps Cards

	1975	1981	1983	1985	1987	1989
Common players	20¢–50¢	17¢	15¢	20¢	40¢	70¢
Common players, #447–#506	NA*	70¢	$1.20	$1.60	$3.25	$8.00
Common players, #507–#576	NA	$1.00	$1.05	$1.40	$3.25	$4.00
Pete Rose	NA	$55	$225	$300	$425	$575
Complete set	NA	$550	$620	$760	$1,500	$3,600

*NA = not available

rising in value from 50 cents to $50 from 1975 to 1979, 1960 Fleer common cards were only rising from 15 cents to $1.

The value of the Ted Williams card is listed because he was the only active player in the set at the time of issue. Ted Williams was a great Boston Red Sox outfielder from 1939 to 1960, though he missed considerable time when he was on active duty in World War II and in the Korean War. Williams was the last player to hit over .400 for a season, finishing at .406 in 1941. He led the American League in home runs four times and won six batting titles. He finished with 521 home runs and a .344 lifetime average. Williams was elected to the Hall of Fame in 1966.

1963 Topps

The 1963 set is a typical Topps set from the 1952–1973 period, in that it was issued in series and its high numbers (those issued later in the season) are scarcer than its low numbers. The set contains 576 cards, including the first Topps card of Pete Rose (#537). Table 6-6 shows the values for the 1963 Topps cards given by price guides over the years.

Card #537 of 1963 Rookie Stars includes Pete Rose as one of four rookies pictured. This card had a huge price increase between 1981 and 1983 as it became apparent that Rose would break Ty Cobb's record and become the all-time hit leader in baseball history. The card

Table 6-7. Price Guide Value Estimates for 1975 Topps Cards

	1981	1983	1985	1987	1989
Common players	6¢	8¢	12¢	15¢	20¢
George Brett	$6	$11	$20	$38	$55
Robin Yount	50¢	$9	$16.50	$21	$35
Complete set	$70	$135	$210	$400	$550

continued to rise in price until Rose eventually did break Cobb's record. Pete Rose had a tremendous career, playing from 1963 through 1986 and managing the Cincinnati Reds from 1984 through 1989, when he was banned for life from baseball because of his gambling activities. Like all retired players, Rose must wait five years after the end of his playing career before he is eligible to be elected to the Hall of Fame. Though his banishment from baseball may have clouded his Hall of Fame chances, most observers feel he'll still be elected.

Even if Rose does have Hall of Fame entry problems, his 1963 Topps card should not lose any value. In the only comparable case of a major star being banned from baseball for life, Shoeless Joe Jackson was banned for his involvement in the 1919 World Series gambling scandal. Jackson has still not been admitted to the Hall of Fame, 70 years after the incident, despite having a .356 lifetime batting average, third highest in baseball history. Even without being in the Hall of Fame, Jackson's cards are still priced as if he were. As an example, his 1914 Cracker Jack card is valued at $1,500.00, second in the set only to Ty Cobb's $1,800.00 card, and well above the value of other Hall of Famers in the set.

1975 Topps

The second consecutive year that Topps issued all of its cards at one time was 1975. Beginning in 1974 and extending through the present, Topps has released its entire set at the beginning of the year. Any of the cards in the 1975 set could be found in any pack of Topps cards in the beginning of the 1975 season. This eliminated the scarcity of high-numbered baseball cards.

Topps tried an experiment in 1975, making two entire sets of its 1975 cards, one in the regular card size and an identical one in a smaller size. The small-sized 1975 cards are referred to as 1975 Topps Minis. The 1975 Topps Minis were only distributed in a few areas of the country and are now quite scarce in comparison to the regular size 1975s. Values for the Minis are approximately double the price of the regular 1975 cards. Table 6-7 shows the values for the regular-size 1975 Topps cards over the years.

Card #228 of George Brett and card #223 of Robin Yount picture those players on their first Topps cards. Since all of the cards were issued at the same time in 1975, those cards are just as common as any other card in the set. The only thing that sets them apart is that they are the first cards of players who went on to become baseball stars.

George Brett has won two batting titles, and he came closer to hitting .400 for a season when he batted .390 in 1980 than had any player since Ted Williams in 1941. Brett looks like a pretty sure bet to make the Hall of Fame when his playing days are over, and the values of his cards reflect this.

The value of Robin Yount's 1975 cards show what a great year can do for a player's cards. Until 1982, Yount had played for eight years as a good shortstop for the Milwaukee Brewers, and his 1975 Topps card was at the 50-cent level. In 1982, Yount had a great year and was chosen MVP for the American League as the Brewers made it to the World Series. Yount had been playing regularly in the majors since he was 19, and collectors suddenly noticed how many hits he had amassed. Since he was still fairly young, collectors realized he had an excellent chance of getting 3,000 hits for his career, which is almost automatic qualification for the Hall of Fame. By 1983, Yount's 1975 Topps card was valued at $9, and it has risen steadily since, even though he has not been able to equal his great season of 1982.

Conclusions

Many more sets can be charted according to value trends, but the charts presented here give a good indication of some of the long-term price trends of the past. What these charts show is that with few exceptions, baseball cards have historically always risen in price over time. The rise in prices for older cards has been dramatic for most baseball cards, with over-1,000 percent gains over a 5- to 10-year period being quite commonplace. These charts also show that the prices for these cards are continuing to rise at a dizzying pace. It is unknown just how high they will rise in the future, but their prices seem fairly strong now and do not show any signs of dropping off.

Though no charts are presented for cards of the 1980s, cards from that decade have been rising steadily in price just as the cards before them have been. It is difficult to speculate on the future of cards from the 1980s, since they were produced in far greater quantities than the cards of the 1970s and earlier times. In addition to the recent cards having been produced in huge quantities, many cases of 1980s cards have been hoarded by collectors and speculators in the hopes of achieving the same type of price gains that have been seen in the past. Because of this, it is unlikely that 1980s cards will ever be as valuable as cards from the 1970s and earlier. It is even possible that cards from the 1980s could actually go down in price in the future as speculators seek to sell off their hoards, and some collectors think this scenario is highly likely.

Profiting from Baseball Cards

Over the past few years, the baseball card business has been booming like never before. There are more baseball card dealers, more people investing money in baseball cards, and even more baseball card companies. Despite their printing enormous quantities, the card companies have had trouble making enough baseball cards to satisfy the demand. Baseball card dealers have had problems getting enough of some baseball card issues for their customers. Prices for older cards have skyrocketed. Card dealers have been advertising in greater numbers to buy old baseball cards, with some ads picturing dealers in a state of desperation willing to throw hundred dollar bills at anyone who will sell them cards. With all of this activity, there is room for collectors and investors to make money in baseball cards if they know what they're doing.

Since they rarely go down in value, baseball cards have always been a good investment. In recent years, the values of most baseball cards have increased substantially. Some cards have experienced huge gains, practically overnight. For example, the 1984 Donruss Don Mattingly card sold for about 2 cents in 1984 and went up in value to about $5 in early 1986.

This was already a very healthy increase, but the card went through the roof in late 1986 and early 1987 and was valued at $85 when the 1987 baseball season started. This calculates out to an increase of over 400,000 percent, a staggering figure. When you consider that banks usually pay about 5.5 percent interest on a savings account, the increase is even more overwhelming.

While the 1984 Donruss Don Mattingly card is one of the more stunning recent examples of how quickly baseball card values can rise, it is by no means a lone case. The 1986 Donruss José Canseco card experienced a similar rise during Canseco's great 1988 season and was valued at over $50 in early 1989. The 1989 Fleer Bill Ripken obscenity card sold for 3 cents out of the pack at the very beginning of 1989, then jumped to over $40 when the obscenity was discovered and publicized in late January of 1989. The 1963 Topps card of Pete Rose went from 1 cent in 1963 to approximately $575 in 1989. The 1952 Topps card of Mickey Mantle went from 1 cent in 1952 to about $3,300 in 1987, and then to $6,500 in 1989. Even the lowest valued cards from the 1984 Donruss set that sold for 2 cents each in 1984 were valued at 12 cents in 1987, a healthy rise of 500 percent in three years. In fact, as you look through the baseball card price guides, it is nearly impossible to find any cards that are worth less today than they originally cost.

The Main Factors Affecting Baseball Card Value

In recent years, four factors have had the most impact on determining the value of a particular baseball card. These four factors are as follows:

- Card condition
- Rookie cards
- Superstar cards
- Rare cards

Card Condition

The condition of a baseball card is probably the most important factor in determining its monetary value. As more people have been getting involved with baseball cards as investments, condition has taken on even greater importance. There has been a lot of dialogue in the baseball card hobby about investment grade cards having to be almost perfect. Some dealers specialize in selling only mint or near-mint condition cards to their customers.

Traditionally, baseball cards have been graded on the following scale:

Card Grade	Description
Mint (MT)	A perfect card. The card has perfectly sharp corners, full gloss on the picture, and no damage whatsoever. The definition of a mint card has been expanded in recent years to also include only well-centered cards and cards with no printing flaws (such as a blurry picture).
Excellent (EX)	The card corners are still fairly sharp, the gloss on the picture may show minor wear from rubbing against other cards, and the card contains no creases. Cards may be a bit off-center. This grade refers to a very nice card with no visible damage that is just not quite perfect.
Very Good (VG)	The corners show some rounding, the gloss on the picture shows some wear, and there may be minor creases. There is minor damage to the card from handling, though there are no major creases or other major types of damage. Still a very collectible card.
Good (GD, G)	Card shows much wear such as rounding of corners, major or multiple creases. The card has

Fig. 7-1. Cards in varying conditions. The left card is in poor *condition because of heavy damage at the top. The middle card is in* good–very good *condition because of rounded corners and a couple of light creases on the right near the top. The right card is in perfect shape, with high gloss and crisp corners, making it a mint condition card.*

Card Grade	Description
	some definite problems, though no intentional damage.
Fair (FR, F)	The card shows excessive wear, such as large and multiple creases, excessive surface wear, small pin or staple holes, slight tearing, some tape damage, added pen or pencil marks, other damage. This card is of questionable value to collectors, although it is still basically intact.
Poor (PR, P)	The card shows major damage. Parts may be torn off, there may be large holes, excessive back damage because of glue or tape removal, major pen or pencil writing, water damage, or other major problems. Not a very collectible card.

Other in-between grades such as "VG-EX" and "Near Mint" are also widely used (Fig. 7-1).

With recent cards, the condition of the card must be nearly perfect for it to be worth anything. There is an almost unlimited supply of mint condition cards for every year of the 1980s, making lower grade cards from those years almost impossible to sell.

With older cards, condition is also very important to value, but it is easier to sell older cards that are not in perfect condition. There are a limited number of older cards that have survived in mint condition. As a result of scarcity and investor interest, the prices for mint condition older cards have been skyrocketing. Because of high prices and limited availability, collectors are often willing to settle for older cards in varying conditions at lower prices.

Card condition also applies to unopened material. It is easier to sell cards in unopened packs, because they carry the illusion of being in mint condition. In fact, cards that come directly from packs often have some damage. The bubble gum contained in packs can stain one card, and the wax used to seal the packs usually stain another. There can also be ma-

Fig. 7-2. The baseball card companies are trying very hard to let collectors know about rookie cards, as these cards demonstrate. 1989 Topps Gary Sheffield, 1989 Score Sandy Alomar, 1987 Donruss Greg Swindell. Topps card copyright The Topps Company, Inc.

chine damage from packing the cards in the packs. The cards can be off-center, bent, creased, or blurry from improper printing. *Most of the cards found in unopened packs are in mint condition, but these other problems can occur.* Even with all of these potential problems, unopened packs are usually sold for prices that assume the cards are in mint condition.

Rookie Cards

In recent years, rookie cards of star players have become very valuable. A rookie card is the first major league card of a particular player. Rookie cards of great players are worth a lot more money than the second card of the same player. In 1989, the value of Mike Schmidt's first card was approximately $200, while his second card was worth only $50. Also in 1989, Reggie Jackson's first card was worth $275, while his second card was valued at $50.

Because of the high value placed on rookie cards, there has been some controversy surrounding which card is truly the rookie card of a particular player. From 1956 to 1980 it was easy to tell which card was the rookie card of a player—it was his first Topps card. Now it is becoming increasingly difficult to determine

the true rookie card of a player. Many different companies are producing a major baseball card set per year. In addition, the major card manufacturers produce update sets in late summer (available only to baseball card dealers and not issued in packs) that include new players that did not appear in their regular sets. Also, there are numerous small baseball card sets produced each year that sometimes contain cards of players before they appear in the major sets. To complicate matters further, there are companies that make minor league sets of cards each year, picturing the players before they appear on major league cards. Card dealers have been known to define cards from all of these sets as rookie cards in order to justify high prices.

A few years ago, *Sports Collectors Digest (SCD)* decided to offer its definition of a rookie card to the public. *SCD* defines a rookie card as the first card of a player in the regular sets produced by the major manufacturers. By this definition, recent players each have a rookie card produced by each of the major manufacturers. *SCD* doesn't consider cards from update sets to be true rookie cards, since those aren't available to the general public. Cards from the small sets were ruled out because

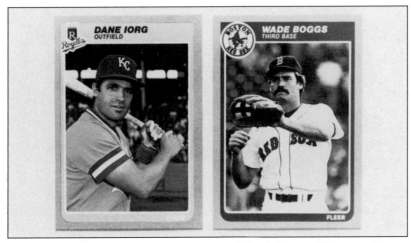

Fig. 7-3. 1985 Fleer cards of Dane Iorg and Wade Boggs. These cards were probably printed in the exact same quantities, yet the Boggs card was valued at $3.75 and the Iorg card at 6¢, according to the 1989 Sports Collectors Digest Baseball Card Price Guide. *The higher value of the Boggs card is based solely on his status as a baseball superstar.*

they are not as widely collected and are often only available regionally. Minor league cards were not considered true rookie cards because the player was not yet pictured with a major league team. The *SCD* rookie card definition seems to have gained acceptance from most collectors (Fig. 7-2).

Rookie cards are printed in the same quantities as any other card in their set. Their sole extra value is based on the player pictured and the fact that it is his rookie card. It has been a fairly recent phenomenon for rookie cards to carry higher values than other cards. Until the 1980s, nobody paid much attention to rookie cards. They were considered basically the same as any other cards. Many people believe that the rookie card craze was started by baseball card dealers (another fairly recent phenomenon) to increase their profits by creating artificial demand for cards that they could readily acquire. This being the case the whole rookie card craze could easily end at any time, but even though rookie card values are highly

inflated it looks like the high values will probably continue for quite awhile, because there are a lot of people actively buying them for investment purposes.

Superstar Cards

Baseball cards of superstar players have always been worth more than those of ordinary players. If you buy baseball cards from the 1930s, you pay a lot more for a card of Babe Ruth than for a card of Eldon Auker. This extra value is basically related to demand. There are equal numbers of cards printed up for each player in most baseball card sets but the cards for star players are always more sought after than those of ordinary players, which raises their value (Fig. 7-3). Most of the cards of the top baseball stars are worth 10 to 20 times the value of a card of a common player from the same set. In cases of the best players and in cases of a great player's rookie card, the value is often considerably higher.

Fig. 7-4. Genuinely rare baseball cards. 1959 Fleer Ted Williams #68, 1949 Bowman PCL Ken Holcombe. The 1959 Fleer #68 card was removed from distribution shortly after it was issued, causing its scarcity. All of the 1949 Bowman PCL cards are rare, as very few were ever distributed.

Rare Cards

Scarcity is always a factor that affects the value of baseball cards or anything that appreciates in value over time. The most valuable baseball card is the T206 Honus Wagner, listed at $95,000 in 1989. A major reason for its high value is that it is a scarce card in a relatively common set of baseball cards. Many baseball card collectors have completed most of that 1910 set, but there are only a limited number of the Wagner cards to go around. The value of this card is particularly high because a lot of collectors have every card but that one, and baseball card collectors like complete sets.

While scarcity is always a factor in baseball card value, it is only one factor. Even though the Wagner card carries the highest value, it is by no means the rarest baseball card. Some sets of baseball cards are so rare that nobody owns a complete set, and some of the cards from these sets are unknown to modern collectors. There are cards from these sets that exist with only one or two known copies. There can be no greater scarcity than a card with only one known copy, yet cards

such as this are usually worth only $1,000 to $2,000 (if they are even for sale, which they seldom are). This is because these extremely rare cards are found in sets that are virtually impossible to complete. If a set cannot be completed, the average collector will not even attempt to collect it, but will instead concentrate on sets that are possible to obtain. With the hundreds of other baseball card sets issued from 1887 to the present, it's not hard to find other sets to collect.

There are many different levels of scarcity for baseball cards. The Wagner card is a case of one card being much more difficult to find than the other cards from the same set. Scarcity can also be seen when looking at entire sets in relation to others. For example, cards from just about any set issued before 1948 are in shorter supply than those issued later. Cards from the 1980s can be found in much greater numbers than those issued in the 1950s through the 1970s. The scarcity level of Topps and other major sets often changes from year to year.

There are very, very few baseball cards from the past 40 years that are rare in the same way the T206 Wagner is rare. The other levels

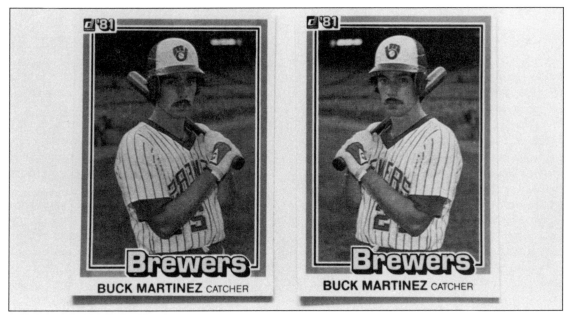

Fig. 7-5. 1981 Donruss variations of Buck Martinez. Card manufacturers often issue cards with reversed negatives like this, but they rarely correct them.

of scarcity, however, must be taken into consideration when evaluating recent baseball card values (Fig. 7-4).

In general, the most common cards of the past 40 years are Topps regular issue cards. These have been produced in the greatest quantity of any cards (although Topps never states how many cards it produces per year). Topps produced cards in from four to seven separate series for the years 1952 to 1973. In almost all of those years, cards from the high-numbered series are worth considerably more than cards from the low-numbered series because the high-numbered cards are scarcer.

There was a surplus of Donruss and Fleer cards produced for the years 1981 to 1983. These cards are still easy to get for a fairly low price. From 1984 to 1987, Donruss cut back on the number of cards it produced. In fact, it did not produce enough cards in any of those years to satisfy demand at the time. As a result, those

cards are now somewhat scarce. Fleer did not print enough cards to meet the demand from 1986 to 1988, and its cards for those years are somewhat scarce.

Baseball cards issued as inserts with various products are usually much more scarce than the major issues are. For example, baseball cards have been found on the back of cereal boxes, inserted with food products, and distributed in other ways as promotional items. These cards often become scarce because a great number of them are purchased by non-collectors and thrown out. On the other hand, there is less demand for these cards than for the major issues. The lack of demand somewhat lowers the value of these cards, despite their scarcity.

Another factor that can cause scarcity is when a card company produces a card with more than one variation. For example, in 1981 both Fleer and Donruss made many errors in their first run of baseball cards. In subsequent printings, many of the errors were corrected, thus creating two or more versions of the same card. Often, there is a scarce version of one of the variations, and this can cause the value to be higher (Fig. 7-5).

It is interesting to note that scarcity has been playing a smaller role in determining the value of a card in recent years than it did in the past. In the 1970s and earlier, scarcity was probably the greatest factor in determining the value of a card. Scarce cards such as the 1949 Bowman Pacific Coast League (PCL) cards were very highly valued in relation to other cards. In recent years, the star player and rookie card factors have had a much greater influence on values than scarcity. While many relatively abundant cards of star players and rookies have shot up in value in the past few years, the values for the 1949 Bowman PCL cards and several other genuinely scarce cards have remained at basically the same level.

Other Value Factors

While condition, rookies, star players, and scarcity are the four main factors determining the value of a card, there are two other important factors that influence values. These factors are *publicity* and *collectibility*.

When a particular baseball card receives a lot of publicity, its value usually increases substantially. The publicity factor usually only comes into play when a card is already valuable because of one or more of the other value factors. For example, when the 1989 Fleer Bill Ripken card was issued, it sold for about 3 cents in wax packs of Fleer cards. When an obscenity was discovered to be pictured on Ripken's bat and Fleer announced that it was creating a new version of the card with the obscenity covered, the value of the card immediately jumped. The value rose to new heights

when the story of the card was carried in mainstream newspapers and magazines across the country. Suddenly, everyone knew about the card and wanted one, regardless of whether or not they had any interest in baseball cards.

As touched on earlier, the collectibility of a card has a direct effect on its value. Even if the other value factors are all in its favor, if a card is deemed uncollectible, its value will drop. Ugly cards and sets that exist only in minuscule quantities are not considered to be very collectible. For example, the M.P. & Co. sets of 1943 and 1949 are extremely ugly, and the crude drawings on the cards do not really resemble the identified player. As a result, very few people bother to collect these cards and their values are fairly low. The 1889 S. F. Hess California League set is so rare that only a few examples are known to exist. Despite their extreme scarcity, individual cards from the set were only valued at $1,000 each in the 1988 *Standard Catalog of Baseball Cards*. The cards are so scarce that few people can even attempt to collect them.

The Whole Picture

Cards that are positively affected by one of the main value factors will see their values increase over time. When a card is influenced by more than one or all of the main value factors, the potential increase can be enormous (Fig. 7-6).

Two of the hottest baseball cards right now are the 1984 Donruss Don Mattingly and the 1986 Donruss Jose Canseco cards. In 1989, the Mattingly was valued at $65 and the Canseco was worth $55 in mint condition. Mattingly and Canseco are now considered true superstars in the baseball card hobby. There is a scramble on for their rookie cards. The Topps and Fleer rookie cards of the players are only worth about half or less of the Donruss card values. The

Fig. 7-6. 1984 Donruss, Fleer, and Topps Don Mattingly rookie cards. The value of the Donruss card is about double the value of the Fleer or Topps card due to relative scarcity. Topps card copyright The Topps Company, Inc.

reason for the big difference between Donruss and the others is that the Donruss cards from 1984 through 1986 were issued in much smaller quantities than the others. Therefore, all four of the main value factors—condition, rookie, superstar, and scarcity—are heavily involved with these cards. In addition, both cards have received a lot of publicity, and they are found in easily collectible sets.

Your Investment Portfolio

If you are interested in baseball cards for investment purposes, there are several different paths you can take. Most investors choose to buy single cards, unopened material, or complete sets. Here's a rundown on what's available, the returns on these items from the past, and probable returns for the future.

Single Cards

When investing in single cards, you have the choice of investing in rookies, superstars, or scarce material.

Rookies

Many people are investing in rookie cards these days, no doubt because of the recent big gains in value for the rookie cards of Pete Rose, Steve Carlton, Tom Seaver, Mike Schmidt, Don Mattingly, Dwight Gooden, Jose Canseco, and other big-name players. It's difficult to get inexpensive quantities of new rookie cards, since everyone seems to be trying to get them. Cards of promising young players are often highly priced, even before the player has made it to the major leagues. Some baseball card dealers specialize in selling large quantities of individual cards, including promising rookies. For example, in early 1987, rookie cards of such promising players as Bo Jackson, Wally Joyner, Jose Canseco, and Ruben Sierra were being advertised for sale for an average of about $2 apiece. These same cards could be purchased for 2 cents each straight from wax packs if you

123

happened to pick the right pack. As you can see, the initial markup for rookie cards is very high. Still, $2 is a small price to pay if the card rises in value like the 1984 Don Mattingly cards did. It's also cheaper and easier to pay $2 each for a large quantity of a single card than to buy cards in packs and try to build up a quantity of a particular card.

If you want to try to make a killing in rookie cards, the first thing you have to do is choose a player you think will make it big and stock up on his cards before they become too expensive. For example, if you invested heavily in Don Mattingly cards in 1984, you would have made a killing over the next several years. One of the big problems is that picking a Mattingly before he hits it big is not too easy to do. Mattingly himself was not drafted by the Yankees until the nineteenth round of the 1979 draft. The best way to choose a player is to become familiar with the potential stars while they are still in the minor leagues and follow their progress closely.

Since there are now several companies producing major sets filled with rookies each year, you also have to choose the manufacturer of the rookie cards you want to buy. The rookie cards that have gone up in value the most are the ones from the scarcest major set for the player's rookie year. Figuring out which set will be scarce while you can still get the cards cheaply is not an easy task. For example, the 1983 Donruss cards were so overproduced that you could buy boxes for half price at the end of the year. For this reason, many collectors in 1984 thought it smart to wait until the end of the year to buy Donruss cards because they would probably get the cards at a lower price. In reality, Donruss cards were much harder to come by that year, and the prices were rising rapidly by the end of 1984. This was something that would have been difficult to foresee at the time.

After you think you've picked the right player and the right card set, you're still at the mercy of the player. Sure, you'll make a lot of money if you pick the right player, but you can lose an equally large amount of money by picking the wrong one. For example, Mark Fidrych had a great first year in 1976, winning 19 games, the Rookie of the Year Award, and the American League ERA title with the Detroit Tigers. Not only did he do well on the baseball field, but he also was able to bring fans into the ballpark in great numbers because of his eccentric habits on the mound. If you were going to invest in anybody's rookie cards that year, Fidrych's cards would have been a likely choice. Yet injuries took their toll, and Fidrych retired with only 28 career wins, far short of expectations. His cards are now selling for little more than when they were issued. Look at Lyman Bostock. Bostock was a great young player who had loads of potential before his career came to a sudden end when he was shot to death. A player's output directly affects his card value. You can never tell what will happen to a player who is currently active. According to the 1989 *Sports Collectors Digest Baseball Card Price Guide,* you have to go back to 1959 to find a Topps set that has common cards that sell for as high as $2 each. If the rookies you invest in today at $2 a card become flops, expect to wait another 30 years or longer to get your money back (Fig. 7-7). Investing in rookie cards can be the fastest way to make a profit in baseball cards, but it is also among the riskiest baseball card investments you can make.

Superstars

You do not have to buy rookie cards to invest in particular players. You can buy cards of star players, regardless of the card's year of issue. Cards of baseball legends such as Babe Ruth and Ty Cobb have been skyrocketing in

Fig. 7-7. Rookie cards of players whose careers ended prematurely: 1977 Topps Lyman Bostock, 1976 Topps Mark Fidrych, 1981 Topps Joe Charboneau. Copyright The Topps Company, Inc.

value over the past couple of years. Cards of Ruth that were available for $100 a few years ago are now selling for over $3,000.

Many nonrookie cards of the stars and superstars of baseball can be purchased for a fraction of the cost of expensive rookie cards. When you buy the card of an established star or a retired Hall of Fame player, there is no risk of that player's performance hurting the card. There is money to be made on star cards of any era if you pick the right players.

Scarcities

Buying single cards from scarce card issues is an investment area that has really only taken off in the past few years. There has been a recent surge in investor interest in mint or near-mint older cards. Some people have been purchasing any mint condition cards they can get from the tobacco sets, the Goudeys, and even the early 1950s Topps cards. The supply of mint cards from old sets is very small, and prices have been rising very rapidly on these in recent years. If you are interested in investing in this area, expect a lot of competition

and a very high initial investment, as inexpensive mint cards are just about impossible to find for any older material.

Unopened Material

One of the best baseball card investments that can be made is in unopened material. Many investors are starting to buy cases of wax packs or boxes of wax packs and leaving them unopened. Unopened material from the past has been selling for very high prices, especially unopened material from sets that contain valuable rookie cards. For example, unopened cases of 1984 Donruss that contain the valuable Mattingly card are selling for close to $4,000. These same cases could be purchased in 1984 for under $200.

Baseball cards have traditionally been sold in sealed packs. The major manufacturers usually issue about 15 different cards in a package for about 50 cents. The packages are sealed, so you don't know which cards you will get in each pack. There are usually 36 packs in a box, with 20 boxes in a case (Fig. 7-8). The cards

Fig. 7-8. Unopened cases, boxes, and packs of baseball cards. Cases shown are a 1986 Topps 20-box wax case and a 1987 Donruss 10-box wax case. Boxes shown are a 1989 Donruss and a 1989 Score wax box. Packs pictured are two from 1984 Donruss and one from 1989 Donruss.

are sold in other ways, too. They are sometimes sold in cases of complete sets, perhaps 15 sets per case; or in rack packs, which are three see-through packs of cards sealed together; or in boxes of unsorted cards without wrappers or gum or anything extra.

There are some good reasons for investing in unopened material, especially cases of unopened packs, and keeping the cases sealed:

• One of the joys of baseball cards is in the opening of the packs to see what hidden treasure might be contained therein. Opening older packs is even more fun. People will be willing to pay a high price in the future for the privilege of opening packs of old cards.

• Each year there are some cards that are worth more than others. If the packs are unopened, future buyers might buy them in the hopes of getting a high-priced card at a discount. For some people, this approach is like trying to hit the jackpot in a lottery.

• Baseball cards are typically packaged in loosely sealed wax packs. In recent years, more and more people are wary of buying packs because of possible tampering. They are afraid of unscrupulous people opening the packs, removing the valuable cards and replacing them with others, and then resealing the packs. With unopened cases, this tampering is a lot less likely, and thus people are less afraid of getting ripped off.

Table 7-1. Approximate Values for Individual Unopened Cases

Year	Manufacturer	Price ($)
1981	Topps	1,450
1982	Topps	1,250
1983	Topps	2,300
1984	Topps	2,100
1985	Topps	2,300
1986	Topps	300
1987	Topps	600
1981	Donruss	700
1982	Donruss	700
1983	Donruss	1,600
1984	Donruss	5,300
1985	Donruss	2,650
1986	Donruss	2,400
1987	Donruss	1,400
1981	Fleer	675
1982	Fleer	700
1983	Fleer	1,300
1984	Fleer	3,750
1985	Fleer	3,750
1986	Fleer	2,225
1987	Fleer	2,175

- With cases, your selling options are much greater. You can sell the cards as an unopened case, or you can open the case and sell the cards as unopened boxes, or you can open the boxes and sell the cards as unopened packs, or you can even open the packs and sell the cards individually. In the future, you can look at the market and decide which option will bring you the most money.
- With cases, you can usually buy at a very good price. Since you are buying in bulk, prices are much lower than if you buy cards in smaller quantities. In the year of manufacture, cases can usually be bought at considerably less than the retail price of the packs.
- With cases, you get a sufficient quantity of cards to make a decent profit. If you buy one card at 2 cents and sell it for 10 cents you make a 400 percent profit, but only 8 cents. If you buy a case at $200 and sell it for $400 two years later, you make only a 100 percent profit, but you make $200.

Table 7-1 lists some approximate values for unopened cases of baseball cards. The original prices for these cases were approximately

Fig. 7-9. A complete set of 1987 SportFlics cards.

the same as the prices for new cases that you can buy now (approximately $200 per case). The values for Table 7-1 are taken from the December 1989 issue of *Tuff Stuff* magazine. As you can see from Table 7-1, the worst you would have done on any case of cards purchased from 1981 to 1987 was to make a modest profit. In most cases the gains are substantial.

The only thing bad about unopened cases is that it appears as if a lot of people are starting to save them, which means that there may be a surplus of unopened cases in the future. There is always the risk that the supply of unopened material will become so great that there will be a glut on the market in the future, thereby driving prices down.

Complete Sets

For a sound investment, almost everyone recommends complete sets of baseball cards. By definition, a complete set contains one of every card issued in a particular set. Complete sets do not have to contain every variation for every card; they must only contain one card for each number in the set. For example, in

the 1979 Topps set there are two versions of the Bump Wills card, one showing the team name as the Rangers and the other showing it as the Blue Jays. A 1979 Topps set would be considered complete if it contained *either one* of these two cards; it does not have to contain both of them. Make sure you know what you're getting when buying complete sets (Fig. 7-9).

Buying baseball cards in complete sets takes the guesswork out of which cards will become the valuable ones in the future by making sure you get all the cards in a set. Sometimes it's hard to predict ahead of time which cards will become valuable, and this approach ensures having at least one of each card. For example, Al Kaline had a rather undistinguished first year in 1954 when he hit .276 with 4 home runs. He would have been an unlikely player to invest in after that year. The next year Kaline won the batting title with a .340 average and hit 27 home runs, going on later to make it to the Hall of Fame. Kaline's first card from 1954 was valued at $550 in 1989. Another unlikely investing choice would have been Bob Uecker. He batted only .200 in a fairly brief career in the 1960s. He later became famous as a comedian and a Miller Lite beer spokesman, leading to a large rise in value for his cards. These examples show how hard it is to predict the future value of individual cards. Someone investing in full sets will automatically have any individual card from the sets that becomes valuable in the future.

When baseball cards are issued, you can usually get a complete set of new cards for $15 to $25. If you take a look at the values of complete sets of the past, it's easy to see how much money you would have made by purchasing them when they were issued. Here's a list of the approximate values for some complete Topps sets from the past in mint condition (according to *The 1989 Sports Collectors Digest Baseball Card Price Guide*):

Topps 1952	$38,000
Topps 1961	4,400
Topps 1967	2,900
Topps 1972	1,150

Topps 1975	550
Topps 1980	140
Topps 1981	80
Topps 1982	75
Topps 1983	85
Topps 1984	85
Topps 1985	90

While this chart shows some of the biggest gainers, every one of the Topps sets issued before 1981 is worth more than $100, and every one issued since is worth more than when it was originally issued. It's hard to say how big the gains of the future will be in newer complete sets. They will probably not be as big as in the past, due to the huge numbers of cards now being produced and to the large amount of investor money that is now entering the baseball card hobby, but complete sets should still bring a good return.

Taking Care of Your Investment

If there is a drawback to investing in baseball cards, it is that they must be safely stored somewhere. This is an important consideration, especially when buying cases or complete sets. The cards must be stored, and it is a good idea to see that they are covered on your household insurance or in a separate policy. If you don't have insurance and there is a theft, a fire, or water damage to your cards, your investment is gone.

Very valuable cards should probably be stored in a safe deposit box at a local bank. It's a shame to have to do this, because it takes away from the joy of looking at the cards, but it does protect your investment.

The best way to store cards in your home is in a dry place, elevated from the floor. There should not be too much weight placed on top of boxes containing cards so they will not be crushed. You should never put rubber bands around groups of baseball cards, because the band often damages some of the cards.

When storing groups of cards, most collectors use customized baseball card storage boxes or binders with plastic sheets. These are both relatively modern inventions, designed to serve baseball card collectors and investors.

Baseball Card Storage Boxes

There are a number of different types of storage boxes designed to hold baseball cards. Many baseball card dealers sell custom, baseball card–sized boxes made of sturdy card-

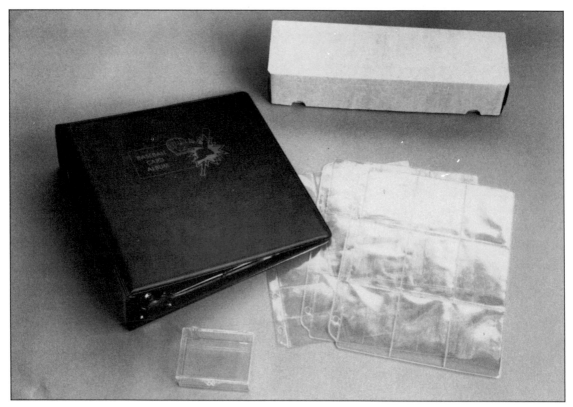

Fig. 7-10. Baseball card storage supplies: a baseball card album and some plastic pages, a corrugated storage box (holds 800 cards), and a small plastic storage box (holds 50 cards).

board. The standard size holds 800 cards, but there are other sizes for different amounts. There are also large wooden boxes and small plastic ones designed specifically for baseball cards. The large wooden boxes are made to store several thousand cards at once. The small plastic boxes usually hold 100 cards or less. The best place to find baseball card boxes is at a baseball card store or through ads in baseball card magazines.

Plastic Pages and Binders

There are many sizes of plastic pages available for baseball cards. Plastic pages contain slots to hold individual baseball cards and are designed to fit in three-ring binders. The standard plastic page holds nine standard-sized baseball cards ($2\frac{1}{2}'' \times 3\frac{1}{2}''$). Almost every baseball card store carries these pages. Some card dealers carry pages with slots for many different sizes of baseball cards, from pages with 18 slots for the small tobacco cards to pages with only one slot for very large cards.

Custom binders for baseball cards are also available. The main difference between custom binders and regular binders is that the custom binders have straight posts to replace the round rings in regular binders, which are important for keeping the pages flat in the binders so that the cards within the pages do not get bent (Fig. 7-10).

Plastic pages are a fairly recent development in the storage of baseball cards and have really revolutionized the baseball card hobby. In the past, there was no real way to display baseball cards easily. At the Metropolitan Museum of Art, the cards from the Jefferson Burdick collection are all mounted in paper albums with the cards pasted onto the pages. Even though this may be the greatest collection of cards in the world, virtually every card has been damaged because there were no plastic pages available in the early 1960s when Burdick was mounting his collection.

There have been some warnings issued about the use of plastic pages for housing baseball cards. In the mid-1980s there were some articles in the baseball card magazines that warned that over time some of the chemicals used in making plastic pages would ooze onto the baseball cards. Since plastic pages have been used for such a short time period, it's hard to tell if this is true or not. So far, there have been no publicized cases of plastic pages damaging cards. If you are going to place many valuable baseball cards in plastic pages, it's probably a good idea to take them out once in a while to inspect them and make sure that they are not being harmed. In addition to plastic pages, there are also available some plastic holders and stands for individual cards, some of which are very thick to protect the cards completely against bending.

Liquidating Your Investment

Some Investment Plans

When investing in baseball cards, you should have a plan on how long you want to wait before liquidating your holdings. The profits you make on paper are all sweeter when the money is in hand. Also, as the money starts to roll in, you may decide to reinvest some of the profits and buy greater quantities of cards for future investments. In any event, here are several investment plans that might be of interest:

- **Plan A.** A good way to realize a quick profit and to set yourself up for a nice profit every year would be to follow a three-year plan. The way to make this plan work is to buy a case of cards from the major manufacturers each year, and then after three years sell off all of the cases from the oldest year. This should bring you a nice profit and will also finance the purchase of cards for the next year. This type of plan can be carried out indefinitely. If you wish, you can use this plan for different quantities of cards or different lengths of time.
- **Plan B.** When you buy cards, set a price at which you want to sell the cards and wait for their value to reach that level. When the level is met, then sell.
- **Plan C.** Buy the cards and hold on to them indefinitely. In general, baseball card prices continue to go up with time. The longer you hold on to them, the more they are worth.

The Sellers' Market

There has always been a ready market for selling old baseball cards, and there is every indication that the market for old baseball cards is still growing. Nothing shows this more than in the number of buy ads that are now appearing in the baseball card newspapers and magazines. Never before have baseball card dealers been clamoring for old cards as they are now. If things continue as they have been, you will have no trouble whatsoever in selling your cards. All you will have to do is to pick a baseball card dealer and ask him what his current buying price is for your cards or pick up a current baseball card magazine and find the dealer with the best buying price for your cards. If you want to maximize your profits, you can run an ad of your own in a baseball card magazine or buy a table at a baseball card show and sell cards as a dealer. You have many choices when you want to liquidate some or all of your holdings.

Selling Directly to Baseball Card Dealers

If you want to sell all or a part of your baseball card collection quickly, there are many dealers that will buy your cards. The only problem with selling cards to dealers is that they will not pay you full price guide (retail) value. Dealers themselves sell the cards for retail, so they cannot afford to pay that amount for your cards. They will generally pay between 30 percent and 50 percent of retail, depending on what type of cards you have. If you have cards that are very easy for them to sell, they'll pay you a higher percentage. Baseball card dealers are the best people to sell your cards to if you want to sell them quickly or if you want to sell all of your cards at once. They are not the best people to sell them to if you want to maximize your profits.

Selling Cards Through the Mail

If you want to try to maximize your profits, you can sell your baseball cards using a mail-order ad. It only costs a few dollars to run a classified ad in the hobby papers. If you want much larger exposure, you can pay a little more and buy a display ad.

When selling via a magazine ad, you can sell your cards for a specified price, or you can run a mail auction. When setting a price for your cards, remember that you are competing with many other advertisers. If you charge too much, you will not get a good response. Mail auctions are mainly used for selling older cards. Most buyers will not bother bidding in a mail auction if they can simply buy the same material from another dealer at a reasonable price.

There are some costs to consider when selling cards through the mail, including advertising, postage, and packing materials. Before placing an ad, you should estimate the amount of material you can sell from the ad and be fairly certain that your sales will pay for the ad and still leave you a good profit. Keep in mind that you might not sell everything you have to offer in the ad. You also have to make a decision about how you will deal with postage costs. Most mail-order dealers add a postage and handling cost to their ordering instructions in their ads, although some add the postage cost into their prices and sell the cards postpaid. You should also use proper packing materials when sending cards through the mail, and you must figure the cost of these materials into your pricing.

If you decide to sell your cards by mail order, be sure to check other ads in the magazines for several issues for cards such as yours. Find out the current market prices for the cards, and see how many competitors you have. These factors could well determine whether or not you should even run an ad. In general, you should have a good grasp of what you're doing being attempting to sell baseball cards through the mail.

Selling Cards at Baseball Card Shows

Selling your cards at a baseball card show gives you a great opportunity to sell your cards directly to baseball card collectors or investors for the full retail price. When you pay to have a table at a show, you are given about eight feet of space to display your cards. Shows are usually held on weekends, when most people are best able to attend.

The main cost to consider when setting up at a show is the table fee. You must be able to make enough money to pay for the table before you can start to make a profit. You need to have a seller's permit, and you are responsible for paying state sales tax for any cards you sell. You will also have to set up displays for your cards. Many baseball card dealers use glass display cases for their valuable cards and plastic pages in binders to display other cards. If you want to display your cards in these ways, consider the cost of the display materials.

There is also the cost of your time and labor. If you sell cards at a show, you will have to remain at your table for the entire length of the show or else get someone else to help out. You will have to establish prices for all the cards you bring, making sure your prices are competitive with the other dealers at the show. Consider also the physical labor of hauling your material from your home to the show and back again.

Selling at baseball card shows is not for the average person. Most of the people involved make a large part of their living selling baseball cards. Unless you have a large amount of material available at good prices, it is possible that you may not even make back your table cost.

A Few Last Words About Selling

When you choose to sell your cards, you will have to make some decisions as to what cards you want to sell and how you want to sell them. For example, you might have cases of cards from a five-year period that you would consider selling. Before selling, you should first take the time to read the ads in the hobby papers for several issues to get an idea of the prices being charged for your cards. You should also check the various ways they are being sold and the prices charged for different selling methods. For example, the market rate for some of your cases might be $500, but the rate for unopened boxes might be $30. That means that you could make $500 by selling the case all at once, or you could make $600 if you opened the case and sold the 20 boxes one at a time. Of course, it's less work to make one $500 sale than it is to make twenty $30 sales. You have to weigh the cost in dollars and in your time.

You must also judge whether it is the right time to sell your cards or if waiting awhile might be better. If you are selling 1990 cards in 1990, you will find a lot of selling competition, since almost anyone can get the cards. On the other hand, the greatest demand for cards of any year is in the year they are produced. Thus, if you choose to sell 1990 cards in 1990, you will have a lot of competition but you will also have a lot of buyer interest. Your prices may have to be somewhat low, but you can probably sell more. If you sell 1987 cards in 1990, there will be less selling competition, since most dealers will have sold their 1987 cards and will be concentrating on selling cards from 1990. You can sell the 1987 cards for a higher price in 1990 than you could have gotten for them in 1987. It is a good idea to think about these and other factors before you sell your cards. Once you sell them, they're gone for good.

The Future

The future looks bright for baseball card collecting. There are more baseball card sets being issued than ever before; interest has never been higher; prices for cards are soaring; and there are more baseball card stores, more and bigger card shows, and more people involved in baseball cards than at any time in history. With everything that is going on in the present, it is important to look towards the future and try to see where all of this activity is heading.

Baseball Card Availability

The most important thing to look at concerning the future of baseball card collecting is the availability of new baseball card sets. If new baseball cards become unavailable in the future, baseball card collecting will drop significantly in popularity. In the past there have been periods of time when baseball cards were unavailable because no companies were issuing them. However, with the tremendous popularity of card collecting today, it is almost certain that many companies will continue to issue cards every year in the foreseeable future. This is good news to baseball card collectors, because as recently as the 1970s there were only a handful of baseball card sets being issued per year.

Shortages

Even with all of the cards being issued these days, there have been baseball card shortages over the past few years. After cards are issued, there is no guarantee that they will be available to the general public. With the quick price rises of some cards these days, people have been snapping up the entire supplies of some issues as soon as they hit the shelves at stores. In an even more ominous development, many of the cards are now being grabbed *before* they ever reach the stores. Because of this, some card sets that are now being issued are unavailable to the general public at their suggested retail price. They are still available, but only from those people that have cornered the market, and not at retail stores. The prices charged are often twice the original retail price or more.

Many collectors who have been buying new cards every year at retail prices are understandably frustrated at having to pay twice the retail price in the year the cards are issued. It wouldn't be so bad if the card companies had just raised prices, but the feeling among collectors is that they are being robbed by unscrupulous card dealers and by card companies that are creating contrived shortages of cards in order to increase their popularity. In response, many collectors are simply not paying the higher prices for new issues, while others are paying them angrily. This situation is creating a lot of ill will in the baseball card hobby.

Reasons for Shortages

There are three main reasons for the recent shortages of baseball cards:

1. There are now a large number of investors involved in the baseball card hobby.
2. There is a lot of panic buying, and dealers are buying up entire supplies of cards as soon as they arrive.
3. Some of the card companies are unwilling or unable to meet the new huge increases in demand for their cards.

Investors

With all of the publicity that has recently been generated about how much money could have been made from investing in baseball cards in the past, it's no wonder that investors are now getting heavily involved in baseball cards. There are people now who are investing thousands of dollars in new baseball cards and then storing them away unopened in the hopes of

making a big profit over the next several years. A huge part of the supply of baseball cards that had been distributed to the general public in the past is now being bought by these investors and stored away before anyone even sees them.

It's easy to see how the supply of cards could be dried up by investors. In past years, the average retail store probably sold one case of cards over the course of the summer. Now investors are buying 10 to 20 cases of cards or more at a time and storing them away. One investor can effectively buy up the supply that has in the past been assigned to 10 or 20 stores. It doesn't take too many investors to dry up the entire supply of cards for every store in the country.

Panic Buying

Since many of the retail stores that carried baseball cards in the past have been unable to get their usual supply of cards because of investors drying up the supply, the stores that do get cards are often getting raided by panic buyers and baseball card dealers. These are people who are not finding cards at the usual stores and are reading about fast-rising prices in the baseball hobby magazines. When they do manage to find the cards at a store at retail prices, they are buying up the entire supply of cards immediately. This effectively dries up any remaining supply of baseball cards from retail stores.

The Card Companies

The card companies could easily print more cards and end the shortage problem themselves, but they don't always choose to do so. There are reasons for their lack of action. One reason is that they want to sell all that they print rather than print more than they can sell.

When Fleer and Donruss first started selling baseball cards in 1981, their cards were quickly gobbled up by a hungry collecting community. For the first few months of 1981, their cards were very difficult to find. Since their cards sold so well, they decided to print more to satisfy the demand. When collectors found the cards available once again, the people who had previously gobbled up the first batch of cards began to panic and started selling off their surplus supply in direct competition with the manufacturers themselves. As a result, the cards became abundant and the manufacturers found themselves with a surplus of cards at the end of the year that they had to sell at greatly reduced prices. This pattern continued through 1983.

In 1984, Donruss decided not to make a second printing of its cards when the first batch ran out. For the first time, there was no surplus of cards to sell off at the end of the year. Donruss probably didn't anticipate that their new policy would create a much greater demand than they could have hoped for, but when the company did realize this, it began using the situation to its advantage. From 1985 through 1987, Donruss increased the production of its cards for each year but kept to the policy of only one print run. Because of this, Donruss virtually guaranteed that it would be able to sell everything it printed. There aren't many companies in the United States that can sell everything they make before they've even made them.

Both Fleer and Donruss limited the number of cards they produced in the mid-1980s and late-1980s. As a result of this limitation and because of the huge increase in demand

for new cards over those years, some of their cards have become relatively scarce. The quantities the companies printed were probably enormous, but the cards are still very hard to get at decent prices. In 1988, Donruss began printing enough cards to satisfy demand once again, and Donruss cards can now be seen at retail stores. It is very likely that Fleer will once again print enough to meet their demand in the near future.

Upper Deck was the first company to try openly to create a shortage atmosphere with its cards. Upper Deck placed many ads in the hobby magazines before its first set of cards was issued in 1989, telling collectors that the company would only print a certain number of cards and that collectors had better get them quickly. Upper Deck ads showed some happy children playing with Upper Deck cards and other children crying because they waited too long to purchase theirs and ended up without any.

Topps has continued with its standard policy of selling cards based on demand. Topps does not limit itself to any quotas of cards each year. As a result, the company has been selling tremendous amounts of baseball cards in recent years. Topps is striving to fill the demand of both investors and retail stores, and it has been doing a good job of making its cards available to everyone, which discourages the panic buyers from cleaning stores out of Topps cards. People know that Topps cards will be available throughout the summer, so there's no real hurry —or panic—in buying them.

Counterfeits

The thought of baseball cards being counterfeited strikes terror in the hearts of all collectors, dealers, and investors. Baseball cards, as well as many other collectibles, derive a large

part of their value from the fact that they are not reprinted after their release period has ended. Even though the major baseball card manufacturers could theoretically print up their old issues, they know that to do so would be to cut their own throats. The manufacturers know that reprinting their cards in later years would render the cards worthless from a collector standpoint. Collectors have never seriously worried about the major manufacturers reprinting their old issues.

Collectors do worry about counterfeits appearing for valuable baseball cards. There have been many cases of baseball card counterfeiting in the past, and it's highly likely that as baseball card values rise, the number of attempts and the quality of the fakes will rise also. Collector Lew Lipset cited the possibility of a counterfeiting scare as one of the reasons he sold his copy of the Honus Wagner T206 card.

Some of the cards that have been unlawfully duplicated in the past include some N172 Old Judge cards from the 1880s, Goudey cards from the 1930s, the 1959 Fleer Ted Williams card #68, the Topps 1963 Topps Pete Rose rookie, the 1984 Donruss Don Mattingly, and the 1984 Fleer Update card of Dwight Gooden. All of these fakes were discovered by knowledgeable baseball card collectors who could see noticeable differences between the originals and the fakes of these cards. It is possible that future counterfeiting attempts will be more difficult to detect. The 1984 Fleer Update Dwight Gooden fake was a particularly ominous case of what can happen. A Fleer employee ran off some unauthorized copies of the cards from the original printing plates. Fleer took action against the employee when it found out what had happened, but this example shows that unauthorized reprints of the highest quality are possible.

In 1987, the Nashville Sounds minor league baseball team reprinted a baseball card set that it had issued in the early 1980s featuring Don Mattingly as a minor leaguer. The new cards contained no markings to indicate that they

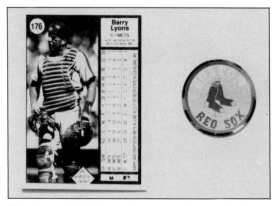

Fig. 8-1. 1989 Upper Deck card back for Barry Lyons and 1989 Upper Deck hologram team logo of the Boston Red Sox. A small diagonal hologram is located near the bottom of the backs of Upper Deck cards.

were reprinted. This action sent shock waves through the card collecting hobby, because the set was becoming very valuable, and suddenly all its value disappeared. Since the Nashville Sounds team is not a major manufacturer of baseball cards, it apparently didn't understand the ethics of baseball card issues. The team either didn't know or didn't care that it wasn't supposed to reprint its old cards. This incident proved that not every manufacturer of cards can be trusted not to print more in the future.

As printing technology improves, so does the chance for successful counterfeits. For example, Topps recently pressed charges against counterfeiters who had used "digital retouching," an advanced computerized printing process, to create high-quality counterfeits. The fakes were of such high quality that they had to be subjected to expensive chemical analysis before they could be positively identified as counterfeits.

A sobering thought for collectors is that just because some attempts at forgery have been discovered, doesn't mean that other attempts will always fail. A trained eye and experience in dealing with the real thing are the best defense against getting burned, but nothing is ever certain.

One company that is trying to make counterfeit-proof baseball cards is Upper Deck. Upper Deck has added holograms to the backs of its cards to try to make counterfeiting more difficult. Because of the holograms, the cards sell for a higher price than Topps, Fleer, Donruss, and Score cards. It will be interesting to see whether collectors will mind paying a little more for counterfeit-proof cards, and whether other card companies will follow suit (Fig. 8-1).

Future Price Trends

Prices for baseball cards have risen beyond what most people expected. The decade of the 1980s brought tremendous growth to the baseball card hobby, and with this growth came escalating values for almost all cards. Knowledgeable baseball card people have differing opinions about how high prices will rise in the future. Some people are even predicting a crash in the baseball card market.

In the long run, there are some cards that will always retain their value. There will always be a demand for older cards, since the supply of these cards is limited. However, it remains to be seen what will happen to the values of cards from the 1980s. Most of the major issues from those years were printed in such huge numbers that there will have to be a lot of new collectors for the demand to ever exceed the supply. The 1980s cards that will probably be worth the most over time are the interesting regionals and minor issues. Those cards are usually overlooked by investors because they can't acquire enough of them to make a sizable investment. Dealers do not always stock them because their money is being spent to purchase the major issues. The main people that are still getting the minor issues are collectors. Large quantities of those cards are not being saved by very many people. This will lead to a scarcity of those issues in the future, and scarcity usually leads to higher prices.

It is very likely that price cycles will develop for baseball cards. In fact, these cycles may have already begun. The only time the baseball card hobby was anywhere near as hot as it was in the late 1980s and is currently was in 1981. There was a lot of hoarding of cards that year. From 1982 through 1986 the hobby cooled down a bit, and people didn't hoard as many cards. Prices are now generally lower for cards issued in 1981 than for cards of any year from 1982 through 1986. The hoarding of 1981 has made those cards more abundant today than cards issued in the several years that followed.

As the values of the mid-1980s cards began to rise dramatically, people began hoarding once again. In 1987, there was once again mass hoarding of baseball cards. Other than Topps cards, baseball cards were rarely seen in retail stores that year, as speculators were buying in large quantities. It is very likely that cards from 1987 will be available in large quanties through the hobby in future years, while cards from the next few years will again be more difficult to find.

Future Directions

As baseball card collecting in America has grown, so has the future potential for new and different directions for baseball cards. Baseball cards are now used regularly as props in major Hollywood movies, from such baseball-oriented films as *The Natural* and *Bull Durham* to other movies with more general themes such as *Mask* and the Academy Award–winning *Rainman.* (Squeamish collectors may not want to watch *Mask,* as actress Cher actually rips a baseball card in half.) Network television shows have also used baseball cards. In the "Magnum" television series, Magnum himself owned a shoebox-full of old baseball cards, which he pulled out on occasion. An episode of the television program "Hart to Hart" was built entirely around a baseball card theme, and it is entirely possible that a major Hollywood movie might use baseball cards as a theme in the future (Fig. 8-2).

Other new uses for baseball cards are developing. A judge accepted baseball cards as part of the bail of a San Diego man who was arrested in the late 1980s. It is entirely likely that baseball cards will be used as collateral for major loans in the future.

Baseball cards are being pictured on a variety of new products. There are now school folders with Topps baseball cards on the covers, as well as T-shirts, sweatshirts, mugs, hats, posters, and other items picturing baseball cards. Baseball cards will probably be pictured on even more products in the near future.

New companies are continuing to issue baseball card sets, and new types of baseball cards are constantly being developed. The SportFlics "Magic Motion" baseball cards added a new dimension to the hobby in 1986. In 1989, LJN Toys issued a set of talking base-

Fig. 8-2. *A 1940 Play Ball card of "Bing" Miller and a card of Roy Hobbs (Robert Redford) from the movie* The Natural. *Note that the Roy Hobbs card is designed to look like a vintage 1940 Play Ball card.*

ball cards in conjunction with Topps. These cards could be placed into a special playing device, and the voice of the player on the card could actually be heard.

Baseball itself is expanding into new terrain. Baseball has been mostly an American sport in the past, but this may be changing. In Japan, baseball has been played professionally for many years, and other countries may soon be playing, too. Baseball was a trial sport at the 1984 and 1988 Olympics and will become a regular sport for future Olympic games. As more countries begin playing baseball, there is the potential for new leagues in other countries. There may even be a real "World" Series someday soon, with countries from all over the globe participating. With all of this baseball activity, there is great potential for new baseball card sets from other countries.

Though baseball card collecting is now in its second century, it may well be that the baseball card hobby is really just beginning.

Reprinted by permission of UFS, Inc.

American Card Catalog
Identification Chart

Here is a complete list of *American Card Catalog* code letters that Jefferson Burdick published in *The American Card Catalog* (taken from the 1960 edition). These letters were used to designate various types of card issues. Numbers were placed after these letters to identify specific card sets. Burdick identified card issues regardless of subject matter, so many of these letters identify sets that do not have to do with baseball. All identifying letters are included here for completeness.

Identification Chart

Identifying Letter	Description of Card Type	Identifying Letter	Description of Card Type
None	19th Century Tobacco	G1-129	Tobacco Banners
A	Tobacco Albums	G130-143	Banners, Non-Tobacco
B	Blankets and Rugs	G145-149	Poster Cards
BC	Cloth Items	G150-159	Albums, Non-Insert
BF	Felt Novelties	G180-181	Movie Stills
C	Canadian Tobacco	G190-195	Advertising Sheet Music
D	Bakery Inserts	G200	Calendars
DC	Canadian Bakery	G300	Cigar Band Labels
E	Early Gum and Candy	H1-186	Currier and Ives
EN	Central and South American Gums	H230-385	Advertising Product and Service
F	Food Inserts	H400-928	Advertising Design Sets
FC	Canada Foods	HA	Pre-1850 Advertising

Identifying Letter	Description of Card Type	Identifying Letter	Description of Card Type
HB	Mechanical Banks	PX	Novelty Metals
HC	Clarks Threads	Q	Stereoscope Cards
HD1-8	Advertising Design Group	R1-346	Gums 1930–1948
HG	Prang Advertising	R401-806	Gums since 1948
HK	Clipper Ships	S	Silks
HL	Liebigs U.S.	SC	Canada Silks
HM	Metamorphic & Mechanical Advertising Cards	SN	Central and South American Silks
HN	Central and South American Advertising	T	20th Century U.S. Tobacco
HP1-6	Advertising Product Groups	T400	U.S. Issued Abroad
HS1-4	Advertising Service Groups	U1	Unclassified Folders
HX	Local Stock Advertising	U301	Match Boxes
J	Soda Cards	UM	Miscellaneous Inserts
K	Coffee Cards	UN	Central and South American Miscellaneous
L	Leathers	UO	Gas and Oil Inserts
M	Periodicals	UT	Theatre Inserts
N	Central and South American Tobacco	UW	Weighing Machine
		V	Canada Candy
NW	Cuba Wrappers	W1-252	Early Album Cards
NX	Miscellaneous Foreign	W401-881	Recent Album Cards
P	Tobacco Pin Buttons	WG	Greeting Cards
PC	Post Cards	Y1-39	Rewards of Merit
PD	Bakery Buttons	Y40-59	Tokens of Affection
PF	Foods Buttons	Y61-79	Name of Calling
PE	Early Candy Pins	Y80-94	Bible Cards
PL	Playing Cards	Y95-100	Scrap Pictures
PR	Recent Gum Pins	Z	Paper Dolls
PU	Miscellaneous Pins		

Baseball Teams (Addresses)

American League

AL Office
350 Park Ave.
New York, NY 10022

Baltimore Orioles
Memorial Stadium
Baltimore, MD 21218

Boston Red Sox
Fenway Park
Boston, MA 02215

California Angels
Anaheim Stadium
P.O. Box 2000
Anaheim, CA 92803

Chicago White Sox
Comiskey Park
324 W. 35th St.
Chicago, IL 60616

Cleveland Indians
Municipal Stadium
Cleveland, OH 44114

Detroit Tigers
Tiger Stadium
Detroit, MI 48216

National League

NL Office
350 Park Ave.
New York, NY 10022

Atlanta Braves
Fulton County Stadium
P.O. Box 4064
Atlanta, GA 30312

Chicago Cubs
Wrigley Field
1060 W. Addison St.
Chicago, IL 60613

Cincinnati Reds
Riverfront Stadium
100 Riverfront Stadium
Cincinnati, OH 45202

Houston Astros
The Astrodome
P.O. Box 288
Houston, TX 77001

Los Angeles Dodgers
Dodger Stadium
1000 Elysian Park Ave.
Los Angeles, CA 90012

American League
continued

National League
continued

Kansas City Royals
Royals Stadium
P.O. Box 1969
Kansas City, MO 64141

Milwaukee Brewers
County Stadium
Milwaukee, WI 53214

Minnesota Twins
Hubert H. Humphrey Metrodome
501 Chicago Ave. S.
Minneapolis, MN 55415

New York Yankees
Yankee Stadium
Bronx, NY 10451

Oakland Athletics
Oakland-Alameda County Coliseum
Oakland, CA 94621

Seattle Mariners
The Kingdome
P.O. Box 4100
Seattle, WA 98104

Texas Rangers
Arlington Stadium
P.O. Box 1111
Arlington, TX 76010

Toronto Blue Jays
Skydome
300 Esplanade West
Suite 3200
Toronto, Ontario, Canada
M5V 3B3

Montreal Expos
Olympic Stadium
P.O. Box 500
Station M
Montreal, Quebec, Canada
H1V 3P2

New York Mets
Shea Stadium
Flushing, NY 11368

Philadelphia Phillies
Veterans Stadium
P.O. Box 7575
Philadelphia, PA 19101

Pittsburgh Pirates
Three Rivers Stadium
P.O. Box 7000
Pittsburgh, PA 15212

St. Louis Cardinals
Busch Stadium
250 Stadium Plaza
St. Louis, MO 63102

San Diego Padres
Jack Murphy Stadium
9449 Friars Rd.
San Diego, CA 92108

San Francisco Giants
Candlestick Park
San Francisco, CA 94124

Baseball Card Publications (Addresses)

There are many excellent publications available for baseball card collectors. The addresses of the leading ones are listed here so that you may contact them directly. Information about each of these publications can be found in Chapter 4 of this book.

Krause Publications
(*Sports Collectors Digest, Baseball Cards Magazine, Baseball Card News, Baseball Card Show Calendar, Baseball Card Price Guide Monthly*)
700 E. State St.
Iola, WI 54990

Baseball Hobby News
4540 Kearny Villa Rd. (Suite 215)
San Diego, CA 92123-1573

Beckett Baseball Card Monthly
3410 Midcourt, Suite 110
Carrollton, TX 75006

Tuff Stuff
P.O. Box 1637
Glen Allen, VA 23060

The Old Judge
P.O. Box 137
Centereach, NY 11720

The Wrapper (non-sport cards)
309 Iowa Ct.
Carol Stream, IL 60188

Baseball Card Reference Books

The books listed here are still in print and are discussed in more detail in Chapter 4 of this book. Many of them can be purchased at your local bookstore. Their publisher addresses are listed here.

Sport Americana Books
Den's Collectors Den
P.O. Box 606
Laurel, MD 20707

Titles include:

- *The Sport Americana Baseball Card Price Guide* by Dr. James Beckett
- *The Sport Americana Baseball Memorabilia and Autograph Price Guide* by Dr. James Beckett and Dennis W. Eckes
- *The Sport Americana Price Guide to Baseball Collectibles* by Dr. James Beckett
- *The Sport Americana Baseball Card Alphabetical Checklist* by Dr. James Beckett
- *The Sport Americana Team Baseball Card Checklist* by Jeff Fritsch and Dennis W. Eckes
- *The Sport Americana T206 The Monster* by Bill Heitman
- *The Sport Americana Football, Hockey, Basketball and Boxing Card Price Guide* by Dr. James Beckett

- *The Sport Americana Price Guide to the Non-Sport Cards* by Christopher Benjamin and Dennis W. Eckes

Krause Publications
700 E. State St.
Iola, WI 54990

Titles include:

- *Sports Collectors Digest Baseball Card Price Guide* by Bob Lemke and Dan Albaugh
- *Standard Catalog of Baseball Cards* by Dan Albaugh

Lew Lipset
P.O. Box 137
Centereach, NY 11720

Titles include:

- *The Encyclopedia of Baseball Cards Volume I—19th Century* by Lew Lipset
- *The Encyclopedia of Baseball Cards Volume II—Early Candy and Gum Cards* by Lew Lipset
- *The Encyclopedia of Baseball Cards Volume III—20th Century Tobacco Cards* by Lew Lipset

Warner Books Inc.
Special Book Sales Division
666 5th Ave.
New York, NY 10103

Titles include:

• *Topps Baseball Cards* by Frank Slocum
• *Classic Baseball Cards* by Frank Slocum

Meckler Books
11 Ferry Lane West
Westport, CT 06880

Titles include:

Baseball Card and Collectibles Dealer Directory by Jim Wright and Jean-Paul Emard

Card Collectors' Company
105 W. 77th St.
New York, NY 10024

Titles include:

The American Card Catalog by J.R. Burdick (reprinted exactly from 1960 edition)

Macmillan Publishing Company
886 Third Avenue
New York, NY 10022

Titles include:

The Baseball Encyclopedia by Joseph L. Reichler

Baseball Card Museums (Addresses)

Metropolitan Museum of Art
The Jefferson Burdick Collection (in the Print Department; viewing by appointment only)
799 Ft. Washington Ave.
New York, NY 10040-1198
(212) 879-5500

The National Baseball Hall of Fame and Museum
Main Street
P.O. Box 590A
Cooperstown, NY 13326
(607) 547-9988

The Larry Fritsch Collection
Museum reopening planned for summer 1990 in the Stevens Point, Wisconsin area at a site to be determined. For up-to-date museum information, contact:

Larry Fritsch Cards
735 Old Wausau Rd.
P.O. Box 863
Stevens Point, WI 54481
(715) 344-8687

Baseball Card Companies
(Addresses)

The Topps Company, Inc.
254 36th St.
Brooklyn, NY 11232

Fleer Corp.
10th and Somerville
Philadelphia, PA 19141

Leaf, Inc. (Donruss)
P.O. Box 2038
Memphis, TN 38101

Major League Marketing (Score and SportFlics)
25 Ford Road
Westport, CT 06880
(203) 227-8882

Upper Deck Company
23705 Via Del Rio
Yorba Linda, CA 92686
(714) 692-1013

Index

INDEX

INDEX